ELITE SERIES

EDITOR: MARTIN WINDROW

# Ardennes 1944: Peiper and Skorzeny

*Text by* JEAN-PAUL PALLUD

*Colour plates by* DAVID PARKER
*and* RON VOLSTAD

OSPREY PUBLISHING LONDON

Published in 1987 by
Osprey Publishing Ltd
Member company of the George Philip Group
12–14 Long Acre, London WC2E 9LP
© Copyright 1987 Osprey Publishing Ltd
Reprinted 1988

*British Library Cataloguing in Publication Data*

Pallud, Jean-Paul
    Ardennes, 1944: Peiper and Skorzeny.—
    (Elite series; 11)
    1. Ardennes, Battle of the, 1944–1945
    I. Title      II. Series
    940.54'21      D756.5.A7

    ISBN 0-85045-740-8


Filmset in Great Britain
Printed through Bookbuilders Ltd, Hong Kong

**Author's note**
All the photographs used in this book are from the
US Army, apart from those captioned 'La Gleize
Museum'. The pictures showing German troops in
action were originally taken by Wehrmacht
photographers and cameramen, but were later
captured by the US Army, some (Poteau,
Kaiserbarracke) as early as the end of December
1944 and the remainder later in 1945.
    This text and selection of illustrations has been
worked up by the author from research material
carried out for his book *Battle of the Bulge* (538 pp,
more than 1200 photographs) published by After the
Battle, London.

## Operation 'Greif'

From the time of the initial planning for 'Wacht am Rhein', the German counteroffensive in the Ardennes, Hitler had turned again and again to the importance of taking bridges across the Meuse before they could be demolished. After going over all kinds of possibilities, he came up with the idea of assembling a special unit to try to capture them. His idea was that this special unit, wearing American uniforms and using American weapons and vehicles, would exploit the surprise and shock, created by the breakthrough, to move forward to the Meuse bridges as if they were retreating Americans.

The leader of this force was to be SS-Sturmbannführer Otto Skorzeny, who had become famous for snatching Mussolini from a mountain-top in Italy the previous year. Just back from another coup for Hitler, the kidnapping of the Hungarian Regent's son and the seizure of the seat of government in Budapest, Skorzeny was summoned to the Führer's HQ at Rastenburg on 22 October 1944. After Hitler had congratulated him and announced his promotion to SS-Obersturmbannführer, Skorzeny listened as the Führer outlined the impending offensive and the part he was to play in it. 'He told me about the tremendous quantity of material which had been accumulated, and I recall that he stated we would have 6,000 artillery pieces in the Ardennes, and, in addition, the Luftwaffe would have about 2,000 planes, including many of the new jet planes. He then told me that I would lead a Panzer brigade which would be trained to reach the Meuse bridges and capture them intact.'

As the offensive was due to start at the beginning of December, this left Skorzeny barely five weeks in which to gather together and train a brand new formation for a special mission. Within four days he had sent his plans for Panzerbrigade 150 to Gen.

**Generalfeldmarschall Walter Model, pictured here during the first week of the offensive, was commander of Heeresgruppe B, the army group charged with Operation 'Wacht am Rhein'. His personal opinion of the whole concept of the operation was far from enthusiastic; he considered it unrealistic—and with reason.**

Jodl (OKW Chief of Staff) with a list of the equipment that would be needed. What he had then in mind was somewhat optimistic—3,300 men in a well-ordered brigade, three battalions strong—yet he was given the immediate go-ahead and promised unlimited support.

On 25 October OKW issued an order asking for suitable men for this operation. The next day Ob.West passed the request down the line to Heeresgruppe B, Heeresgruppe G, Luftwaffen-Kommando West, Marine-Oberkommando West, and even to XXX.Armeekorps (in charge of the operational launching of V-weapons in the Netherlands)—in fact to every headquarters on the Western Front. This widespread search for recruits who had 'knowledge of the English language and also the American dialect' was highly prejudicial to the secrecy of the operation and the request soon became known to the Allies, as confirmed in a

The men upon whom the whole gamble depended—and even in the last months of the war, a force to be reckoned with: Waffen-SS mechanised infantry. These machine gunners from one of the four SS-Panzer-Divisions committed to 'Wacht am Rhein' wear the SS-pattern 1944 four-pocket camouflage uniform. The foreground soldier is carrying an MG 42 and a slung spare barrel; another spare is carried, in the ochre canister, by the man behind the gunner's right shoulder.

report by First Canadian Army on 30 November.

Equipping the brigade called for tanks, self-propelled tank destroyers, armoured personnel carriers, trucks and jeeps, plus weapons and uniforms—all of American origin. Certain items of captured equipment may have been fairly plentiful but this was not likely to make them any easier for Skorzeny to obtain: we may imagine that front-line units felt reluctant at the thought of having to part with precious transport. Hence, on 2 November, Skorzeny wrote to the Chief-of-Staff of Ob.West, Generalleutnant Siegfried Westphall, to draw his attention to the fact that while the necessary equipment undoubtedly existed, because the troops were unaware of why it was actually wanted they might well fail to hand it in. A week later Ob.West

was asked to find, with the appropriate ammunition, 15 tanks, 20 armoured cars and 20 self-propelled guns; 100 jeeps, 40 motorcycles and 120 trucks, as well as both British and American uniforms. Under the codename 'Rabenhügel' their requisition was divided between the three Army groups: Heeresgruppe G was required to furnish eight tanks and 20 jeeps, Heeresgruppe H two tanks and 50 jeeps, and Heeresgruppe B five tanks and 30 jeeps, to be delivered promptly to Grafenwöhr, the location of the new brigade's training camp.

Disappointed at what 'Rabenhügel' had turned up, Skorzeny made his feelings known in a telegram to Ob.West on 21 November, sent under his codename of 'Solar', in which he complained of the dearth of American equipment arriving at Grafenwöhr. The monthly summaries for the allocation of armour reveal the way in which he had to make do with German substitutes to bolster the meagre number of American fighting vehicles which came in. Five Panthers were recorded as being allotted to 'Rabenhügel' on 19 November; five StuGs and six armoured cars (Pz.Späh.Wg.) to Panzerbrigade 150 on 24 November; and six medium armoured personnel carriers (mSPW) to 'Rabenhügel' on 27 November.

A full report sent to Ob.West in November by one of Skorzeny's aides detailed the problems encountered in fitting out the unit, and stated that the target date for its organisation could not be met. No more than 57 of the 150 cars that were required had materialised, and 74 of the 198 trucks. There were five tanks, all German, and eight armoured cars, six of them German; moreover, the report suggested that the vehicles sent to Grafenwöhr could not have been chosen with too much care, as a third of them suffered from mechanical defects and needed five or six days in the repair shops. Of just two Shermans which had materialised, one was out of action with a defective engine, and the other was presumably unserviceable too, as neither of them appeared on the list of available tanks in the report.

At the same time the brigade had been flooded with items from units possessing Polish or Russian

## Panzerbrigade 150

(Strength as it appeared on a document dated 25 November, 1944. In the field, by 20 December, it would be far less powerful.)

Brigade staff with
a recce platoon and
a signals platoon

*Kampfabteilung 2150*
(1st Battalion)

—Signals platoon

—1. Kompanie: 22 Panthers

—2. Kompanie: Panzergrenadiers on half-tracks
  Total of: $\begin{cases} 2 \times 80 \text{ mm mortars} \\ 2 \times 75 \text{ mm guns} \\ 2 \times 20 \text{ mm guns} \end{cases}$

—3. Kompanie: recce troops on armoured cars
  mounting 18 × 20 mm guns

—4. Kompanie: infantry on trucks
  with 2 × 80 mm mortars

—5. Kompanie: as 4. Kompanie

—6. Kompanie: as 4. Kompanie

—7. Kompanie: as 4. Kompanie

—8. Kompanie: anti-aircraft unit
  with $\begin{cases} 6 \times 88 \text{ mm Flak} \\ 3 \times 20 \text{ mm Flak} \end{cases}$

*Kampfabteilung 2150*
(2nd Battalion)

—Signals platoon

—9. Kompanie: 14 StuGs

—10. Kompanie: recce troops on armoured cars
  mounting 16 × 20 mm guns

11. Kompanie: infantry on trucks
  as 4. Kompanie

—12. Kompanie: as 4. Kompanie

—13. Kompanie: as 4. Kompanie

—14. Kompanie: as 4. Kompanie

—15. Kompanie: anti-aircraft unit:
  as 8. Kompanie

—Combat Engineer Company 2150
  with 2 × 80 mm mortars

—Artillery Battery 2150
  with 6 × 105 mm howitzers

—Bridge Building Column 2150
  with 60-ton capacity

Otto Skorzeny, promoted to SS-Obersturmbannführer (lieutenant-colonel) and given command of Panzerbrigade 150 by Hitler in person at Rastenburg on 22 October 1944. He was to find the original concept of the covert unit, uniformed and equipped as Americans, impossible to fulfill due to the shortage of suitable vehicles.

equipment and with little idea of what the request was all about, all of these being 'absolutely useless for our mission', added the report—which also commented that the brigade was still short of 1,500 American steel helmets, and that a number of American uniforms delivered under 'Rabenhügel' were summer issue. Despite all these problems, at least it could be reported that the wireless equipment was suitable, that the morale and the physical condition of the troops were good, and that there were a sufficient number of 'combat interpreters for the special missions'.

How these linguists had been obtained was another story, as Skorzeny was later to write: 'We employed a number of language experts who divided them into categories, according to their knowledge of English. After a couple of weeks the result was terrifying. Category one, comprising men speaking perfectly and with some knowledge of American slang, was ten strong, and most of them were sailors, who also figured largely in category two. The latter comprised men speaking perfectly, but with no knowledge of American slang. There were 30 to 40 of them. The third category consisted of between 120 and 150 men who spoke English fairly well; and the fourth, about 200 strong, of those who had learned English at school. The rest could just about say "Yes". In practice it meant that we might just as well mingle with the fleeing Americans and pretend to be too flurried and overcome to speak.'

Faced with the realities of the situation, Skorzeny had been obliged to scale down his ideas for Panzerbrigade 150 from three battalions to two; and he decided to assemble 150 of the best English-speaking volunteers into a commando unit, 'Enheit Stielau'.

# Panzerbrigade 150

With the brigade structure scaled down to two battalions, each of them was to have four companies of infantry, one anti-aircraft platoon, one company of recce armoured cars and one company of Panzers; the latter was to be equipped with 14 StuGs in the second battalion and with 22 Panthers in the first battalion, which was to have an additional company of Panzergrenadiers. The brigade was to have one battery of self-propelled artillery, one company of engineers and one bridge-building column.

Skorzeny called upon his own specialist units, namely a company of SS-Jagdverbände Mitte and two from SS-Fallschirm-Jäger-Abteilung 600. Since there was no possibility of welding together in the time available an efficient force comprised of volunteers drawn from all branches of the Werhmacht, he asked for, and was given, some regular units for stiffening, which were attached to the SS-Jagdverbände for the duration of the mission. The brigade thus received two Luftwaffe parachute battalions previously attached to Kampfgeschwader 200 (and then known as Sonderverbande Jungwirth), and 7.Panzer grenadier-Kompanie. Tank crews were provided by 4.Kompanie of Panzer-Regiment 11 (6.Panzer-Division); Panzerjäger crews from 1.Kompanie of schwere Panzerjäger-Abteilung 655; and recce armoured car crews from 1.Kompanie of Panzer-Aufklärungs-Abteilung 190 (90.Panzergrenadier-Division) and 1.Kompanie of Panzer-Aufklärungs-Abteilung 2 (2.Panzer-Division). Gunners came from Artillerie-Abteilung I/40, and their weapons from the artillery units of the Führer-Grenadier-Brigade. The brigade staff

**Despite Skorzeny's difficulties, the effect of the rumoured presence of the 'Greif' commandos behind US lines was to be widespread and far-reaching. These MPs of the 84th Infantry Division are checking the identity of vehicle drivers at the Baillonville crossroads.**

came from Panzerbrigade 108, and the two battalion staffs were made up from experienced members of Panzerbrigade 10 and Panzerbrigade 113. Altogether, with other specialist units of engineers and transport, the number of men assembled at Grafenwöhr was about 2,500, some 800 less than had been hoped; about 500 were Waffen-SS, about 800 Luftwaffe, and the rest Heer.

The amount of equipment received at Grafenwöhr was far from what had been hoped; and Skorzeny later explained how they had only four American scout cars, about 30 jeeps and about 15 genuine American trucks, and that he 'had to make up the difference with German vehicles. The only common feature of these vehicles was that they were all painted green, like American military vehicles.' In the matter of weapons things were even worse:

**The capture of superior American clothing during bitter winter weather inevitably led to its being worn by some German soldiers; and in the aftermath of 'Greif', equally inevitably, any soldier who allowed himself to be captured so dressed invited summary execution. This grenadier in American kit was shot at Hotton on 26 December.**

there were only enough American weapons to equip the commando company. Skorzeny had to modify his plans once again, and the brigade evolved into a three-Kampfgruppe unit, each one led by a front-line commander on loan for 'Greif': Kampfgruppe X under SS-Obersturmbannführer Willi Hardieck; Kampfgruppe Y commanded by Hauptmann Scherff; and Kampfgruppe Z led by Oberstleutnant Wolf. Each had the same basic organisation: a small staff, three companies of infantry, two Panzergrenadier and two anti-tank platoons, two heavy mortar platoons, an engineer and a signals platoon, and a vehicle repair unit; in addition Kampfgruppe X and Y each had a Panzer company. The former was issued with the five Panthers manned by the crews provided from Panzer-Regiment 11, and the latter the five StuGs crewed by the men from schwere Panzerjäger-Abteilung 655. To resemble the shape of the American M10 tank destroyer, the turrets and hulls of the Panthers were disguised[1]

[1] See plans, Osprey Vanguard 21, *The PzKpfw V Panther*.

with thin sheet metal, including a distinctive rear turret overhang and the cupola was removed. Like almost everything of Skorzeny's that moved, the phoney 'M10' tank destroyers and StuGs were given Allied five-pointed stars; but for a so-called American outfit the brigade had a definite German look about it! There was a single Sherman available on the eve of the attack, the other having finally packed up for good with transmission trouble as the brigade assembled in Eifel; and very few of his men could actually speak passable English or were convincingly kitted out as Americans.

Training continued at Grafenwöhr; here, too, the unavoidable secrecy had its drawbacks since Hardieck, Scherff and Wolf could not be taken fully into their CO's confidence at this time, and Skorzeny was the only one who knew about the offensive. Extravagant rumours multiplied around the camp, and Skorzeny decided not to try to stamp them out: if they sent any Allied agent barking up the wrong tree, so much the better. Among these rumours was one to the effect that the brigade was to dash right across France and relieve the besieged garrison of Dunkirk or Lorient; and another was that the brigade was to march on Paris and snatch the entire Allied supreme command. It was not until 10 December that even the Kampfgruppe commanders were aware of the actual plans for the brigade; in an interview after the war Skorzeny detailed these plans:

'The mission of the brigade was to seize undamaged at least two Meuse bridges from among the following possibilities: Amay, Huy or Andenne. This action was to be initiated when the attack of the Panzer units reached the Hohes Venn, roughly on a line running north-east and south-west from Spa. At that time my troops were to move forward at night and reach our objective six hours later. It was planned originally that the attack would reach the Hohes Venn on the first day and that we would move out that night. The plan could be carried out only when the area of the Hohes Venn had been reached, because it was necessary to move forward with complete surprise and without having to fight. The three groups were then to move on parallel routes towards these bridges. Radio communications were to be used between groups in order that they might shift if resistance were encountered.'

American MPs tie Unteroffizier Manfred Pernass to the execution stake at Henri-Chapelle at dawn on 23 December. Pernass and two other members of Skorzeny's 'Einheit Stielau'—Oberfähnrich Günther Billing and Gefreiter Wilhelm Schmidt—were captured together wearing US Army uniforms, and were subsequently executed together.

The problem of recognition by friendly troops was vitally important, and all the forces engaged in Operation 'Greif' were to try to identify themselves: they would paint white dots on houses, trees and roads used by them; the unit's vehicles were to display a small yellow triangle at the rear, and the tanks were to keep their guns pointing at nine o'clock; the men had to wear pink or blue scarves and take off their steel helmets; at night recognition was to be made by flashing a red or blue torch.

9

## The Commandos' mission

The best of the English-speaking volunteers were selected for 'Einheit Stielau', the commando unit; but even if they could speak English, none of them had any experience of undercover operations or sabotage. 'In the few weeks at our disposal', commented Skorzeny, 'we could hardly hope to teach them their job properly. They knew the perils of their missions and that a man caught fighting in enemy uniform could be executed as a spy. They were clearly animated by the most glowing patriotism.' They were given courses in demolition and radio techniques; they studied the organisation of the US Army; they learned to recognise American rank badges and American drill; some of them were even sent to prisoner-of-war camps in Küstrin and Limburg to 'refresh' their English through contact with American prisoners.

Wearing American uniforms, carrying American arms and equipment, and travelling in jeeps, the commandos were to be sent on three different missions:

Demolition squads of five to six men were to blow up bridges, ammunition and fuel dumps.

Reconnaissance patrols of three to four men were to reconnoitre in depth on either side of the Meuse, and radio back what they could see, as well as passing on fake orders to any units they met,

Wolf in sheep's clothing: a Sturmgeschütz of Kampfgruppe Y, Panzerbrigade 150, painted as a vehicle of Co.C, 81st Tk.Bn.; note peculiar side skirts, and white stars on skirt, superstructure and frontal armour. This vehicle was abandoned in this field at Géromont. (La Gleize Museum)

reversing road signs, removing minefield warnings, and cordoning off roads with white tape to mark non-existent mines.

'Lead' commandos of three to four men would work closely with the attacking divisions, their main aim being to disrupt the American chain of command by cutting telephone wires, wrecking radio stations and giving out false orders.

According to Skorzeny, the highest American rank used was that of colonel, but seniority of rank was irrelevant: from being Obergefreiter Rolf Meyer the lance-corporal found himself promoted to Second-Lieutenant Charlie Holtzmann; Leutnant Günther Schiltz ended up as Corporal John Weller, and so on.

## Into action

Panzerbrigade 150 had reached its assembly area near Münstereifel on 14 December, moving at night. On the afternoon of 16 December it moved out, and the three battle groups advanced behind the attacking divisions to which they were assigned: the 1.SS-Panzer-Division, 12.SS-Panzer-Division and 12.Volks-Grenadier-Division. The units were placed at the rear of the leading elements of the divisions, with the aim of moving around them on side roads once the objective, the Hohes Venn, was reached. Like most of the units in the area, Panzerbrigade 150 became clogged up in the great snarl of vehicles around Losheim and they were never near the head of the columns where it was intended they should be. SS-Obersturmbannführer Willi Hardieck, the commander of Kampfgruppe X, was killed by a mine that day, whereupon SS-Hauptsturmführer Adrian von Foelkersam took over.

When the leading elements of I.SS-Panzerkorps failed to reach the projected starting point for Panzerbrigade 150's units in the first two days, Skorzeny realised that the whole plan was doomed. Also, unknown to him, Operation 'Greif' was no longer a secret as a document outlining the elements of subterfuge of the operation, if not its aims and objectives, had been captured by the US 7th Armored Division near Heckhuscheid.

On the night of 17 December Skorzeny attended a staff conference at 6.Panzer-Armee headquarters, and suggested that his three battle groups be combined and used as a normal army unit. This was agreed; he was ordered to assemble his units south of Malmédy, and to report to 1.SS-Panzer-Division headquarters in Ligneuville in order to co-ordinate the brigade's movements. As part of a general assault launched by the corps, Panzerbrigade 150 was given the task of taking the key road junction of Malmédy; on 'Rollbahn C', it had lain to the north of the route assigned to Kampfgruppe Peiper. The attack was intended to get in behind the American positions on the Elsenborn ridge, thereby assisting 12.SS-Panzer-Division (still battling to the east to get beyond Butgenbach), and to free 'Rollbahn C' to support Kampfgruppe Peiper, now in difficulty to the west.

In planning his attack Skorzeny relied upon the information brought back by a commando team which had unintentionally entered Malmédy on 17 December. At that time roadblocks held by the 291st Engineers were all that barred his way; now, unknown to him, the town was defended by the 120th Regt. of the 30th Infantry Division, plus the 99th Infantry Battalion. Bridges and railway viaducts had been prepared for demolition, and mines had been laid.

## The battle of Malmédy

By the afternoon of 20 December Kampfgruppe X and Kampfgruppe Y had gathered near Ligneuville, but Kampfgruppe Z was still absent and could only be considered as a reserve for the next day's attack. Skorzeny planned a two-pronged attack: Kampfgruppe Y was to attack on the right flank along the N32 from Baugnez, and Kampfgruppe X on the left flank from Ligneuville along secondary roads. As he had neither artillery nor a powerful unit, Skorzeny hoped for a surprise attack:

Another Sturmgeschütz of Kampfgruppe Y, abandoned beside the N32 at Géromont; it was photographed on 15 January, while Lt. John Perkins, Cpl. Peter Piar and Pte. Calvin DuPre of the 291st Combat Engineers removed a boobytrap from it.

This Panther/M10, coded 'B5' as a vehicle of Co.B, 10th Tk.Bn., was disabled at Malmédy by Pte. Francis Currey, US 120th Infantry, with a bazooka. Currey was to be awarded the Congressional Medal of Honor for his bravery on 21 December.

but this was out of the question, for one of his men had been captured on the afternoon of 20 December and had spoken of a strong attack that was to be launched the following morning. Intelligence had just enough time to send out a warning of the forthcoming attack to the front-line regiments late that evening.

Early on the morning of 21 December Hauptmann Scherff launched his Kampfgruppe Y along the N32 from Baugnez towards Malmédy. The advancing grenadiers were checked by the outposts of 120th Regt., and were soon hammered by such a tremendous artillery barrage that Scherff decided to break off the attack and withdraw to the start-line.

On the left flank Kampfgruppe X had committed two companies of infantry supported by the five disguised Panthers. Moving from Ligneuville through Bellevaux and attacking along the Route de Falize, they struck the positions defended by 3rd Bn., 120th Regt. west of Malmédy at 4.30 am. At the bottom of the hill part of the column continued up the road towards Malmédy, while the main body turned left onto a small road leading across a field to the Warche River bridge and 'Rollbahn C'. Somewhere in the field the Panzers hit an American trip-wire, setting off flares; and suddenly the whole area was lit up by dozens of them, revealing the attack in a brilliant glare of light.

On the Route de Falize the Panthers moved towards the town, guns blazing; but the leading tank hit a minefield in front of a railway bridge and brewed up. From positions along the embankment

above B Co., 99th Infantry Bn. opened fire on the other Panzers as they manoeuvred around their stricken companions, and on the grenadiers who were now charging this embankment. Several times they reached the foot of it, but could get no further. Again and again machine gun crews tried to set up their weapons right in front of the embankment, and paid a fearful price. Artillery emplaced on the hills on the northern bank of the Warche shelled the area; and the use of new proximity-fused shells, set for air bursts, caused some panic among troops who were accustomed to shells that exploded on impact. After two hours of fierce fighting the assault died down and the grenadiers slowly fell back. Their dead littered the area, and the disabled Panther was now blazing, sending up sparks which flickered across the pre-dawn sky.

The Panthers with the main body had opened fire immediately they were caught in the glare of the flares. Within minutes tank destroyers had checked them from behind a house near the bridge. This house was the command post of a platoon of the 823rd TD Bn., attached to the 120th Regt., and it soon became surrounded by the attacking grenadiers. Trapped inside were men from the TD unit, from the 291st Engineers, and a handful of infantry from K Co., 120th Regt.: about 30 of them all told, positioned at every window and putting out rifle and bazooka fire. The grenadiers reached the house and threw grenades into the basement before being forced to retire, but by this time the advancing Panzers had passed the house. One of them took up a position to cover the bridge, and from there it opened fire against the house. All the gunners manning the tank destroyers outside were now dead. It was during this battle that a member of K Co., 120th—Pte. Francis Currey—won the Medal of Honor. Picking up a bazooka and dashing across the exposed road to get hold of some rockets, he returned and loaded the bazooka for Pte. Adam Lucero, who then blasted away at a Panzer's turret. Once the Panther was stopped Currey went out alone with the bazooka; shot up a house occupied by grenadiers; stalked three more Panzers with anti-tank rifle grenadiers; and then turned a half-track machine gun against the same house to give covering fire so that some TD men could make a break for it.

At about 10.30 am the fog that had settled over

the area in the early morning suddenly lifted, bringing the action near the bridge into view from the men on the railway embankment. Trapped inside the house, a handful of defenders continued to hold out, but now started to come under fire from the embankment, as it was thought that the house was in German hands. The Panther at the bridge was hit, and the crew scrambled clear from the turret; as they ran up the road, seeking shelter, four of them were cut down by American riflemen, the fifth remaining hidden in a nearby house until captured later.

The American artillery had put down an overwhelming 3,000 shells by the time the fighting slowly subsided during the afternoon. Skorzeny had been watching from the hilltop on the Route de Falize since daylight and was dismayed to see his Panzers embattled and the advance making no headway beyond the bridge. The Panzers that were left fought on, and covered the grenadiers as they slowly disengaged; Von Foelkersam, the commander of the attack, finally came back himself, limping badly and leaning on the arm of a medical officer: he had been wounded in the backside—a painful if not exactly glorious wound!

By mid-afternoon the brigade was back on the crest of the hill south of the Warche valley. American shells were now landing thick and fast on

the brigade's positions and, as Skorzeny was making his way to Ligneuville to 1.SS-Panzer-Division's headquarters, a piece of shrapnel struck him in the face, almost causing him to lose an eye. Kampfgruppe Y made another attempt east of Malmédy in the small hours of the following morning, 22 December, but the outposts of the 120th Regt. were ready and the German column had to retreat. At 2.00 pm the 291st Engineers brought the immense, stone-arched railway bridge on the N32 crashing down, completely blocking the road west of Malmédy. The bridge carrying the railway over the Route de Falize was also blown, as was the Warche bridge west of Malmédy.

No action developed on 23 December until just after 2.00 pm when American aircraft appeared over Malmédy. From the hills south of the town some German anti-aircraft guns opened up without effect. Some time later another flight of aircraft arrived and, to the horror of those below, their bombs were unloaded on Malmédy, killing many civilians and Americans in the heart of the town. Frantic messages were sent to various headquarters stating that Malmédy was not in German hands.

**This Panther/M10 coded 'B10' made an unplanned entry into the café at La Falize; this photo gives a clear view of the clever general similarity to the American vehicle which was achieved with cladding plates—note that even the spare track links are attached in 'American style'.**

'B7', the only Panther to reach the northern bank of the Amblève at Malmédy. It was stopped only 50m from the bridge by a bazooka round in the engine compartment. The crew ran for safety across the bridge, but all were cut down by American fire except the radio operator, Obergefreiter Karl Meinhardt, who remained hidden for several days before being captured. (La Gleize Museum)

They were told that a terrible mistake had occurred which would not happen again: it did, during the next two days. These bombings, which resulted from the confusion then prevailing, and the very poor communications, killed about 300 civilians (the official figure being 202) and an unknown number of American soldiers. From where Skorzeny was positioned on the hills south of Malmédy, he had been puzzled by these raids; seeing American aircraft return, he thought the town must be in German hands, although he wondered which unit could have taken it.

Panzerbrigade 150 remained in the line until 28 December, when it was relieved by elements of the 18.Volks-Grenadier-Division. After withdrawal the brigade went to Schlierbach, east of Saint-Vith, and then moved by train to Grafenwöhr, where it was disbanded and the troops returned to their own units, as planned. Ob.West reported that the process had been completed by 23 January 1945. Skorzeny estimated that the brigade's losses in killed, wounded and missing amounted to 15 per cent of its original strength; most of them he attributed to artillery fire and air attack.

## The Commandos' fate

In a US Army interview in August 1945, while describing the activities of 'Enheit Stielau', Skorzeny said: 'We actually sent out four groups of reconnaissance commandos and two groups of demolition commandos during the first few days of the attack. In addition, one group of lead commandos went with each of the following divisions: 1.SS-Panzer-Division, 12.SS-Panzer-Division and 12.Volks-Grenadier-Division. Also, one unit went with each of the three groups of Panzerbrigade 150. Of the 44 men sent through your lines, all but eight returned. The last men of the commando units were sent through the lines on 19 December. After this, the element of surprise being lost, normal trips were made, the men wearing German uniforms.'

It is very difficult to ascertain which among all the feats credited to Skorzeny's men are genuine. Actually, it was not a rare practice to send out camouflaged reconnaissance teams behind the enemy lines; because of the psychological impact of Skorzeny's Operation 'Greif', virtually every instance of this was attributed to his men. Another explanation for the inflated number of missions attributed to the commandos lay in the fact that German Infantry often salvaged every article of comfortable American kit they could find, as the quality of German clothing had fallen so low by the fifth year of the war; thus they might well be captured or killed wearing an American field jacket or greatcoat. Post-war literature abounds with incredible stories, each more extraordinary than the last, so that it is impossible to tell which among the purportedly eye-witness accounts can be taken as gospel—the more so that Skorzeny himself was not above embellishing the details of his exploits.

Among these accounts, there are reports from Skorzeny about one team entering Malmédy on 16 December, and about another which convinced an American unit to withdraw from Poteau on that same day; a Belgian, M. Pierre Rupp, told of a reconnaissance at Ligneuville on 16 December by a German dressed as an American officer; Sgt. Ed Keoghan of the 291st Engineers reported that one team had changed the road signs at Mont-Rigi on 17 December; Sgt. John S. Myers told of one team killed near Poteau on 18 December when they betrayed themselves by claiming to be cavalrymen 'from E Company'—the US cavalry used the term 'troop' instead of 'company'; and Leutnant Collonia and Feldwebel Heinz Rohde described after the war their trip in a jeep to the Meuse. . .

All the same, on the basis that one of their prime aims was to create chaos and confusion behind the enemy lines, the 'Greif' commandos were, for their number, incredibly successful. So great was the resulting consternation that the Americans saw spies and saboteurs everywhere. The team that was responsible for creating the biggest scare of all was the one captured at Aywaille on 17 December when its members—Oberfähnrich Gunther Billing, Gefreiter Wilhelm Schmidt, and Unteroffizier Manfred Pernass—failed to give the correct password. It was Wilhelm Schmidt who gave credence to a rumour that Skorzeny was out to capture Eisenhower and his staff. They were given a military trial at Henri-Chapelle, were sentenced to death, and were executed by firing squad on the morning of 23 December. One of the figures commonly quoted in accounts of the operation is that of 18 men having been court-martialled and shot at Henri-Chapelle or Huy; we have identified 13 of these, and the figure of 18 is certainly precise.

# Kampfgruppe Peiper

On 6 December, the plan for 'Wacht am Rhein' was presented to the 6.Panzer-Armee in a map exercise at Brühl. Besides Generalfeldmarschall Walter Model, commander of Heeresgruppe B, and his chief-of-staff, the Army's corps commanders were also present with their chiefs-of-staff and the divisional commanders. The details of the Army's mission were disclosed, and the rôle of the Panzer divisions was emphasised: they were not to be used in the initial breakthrough, and neither the situation on the flanks nor the Americans' possible retention of large towns were to slow down their drive to the Meuse. On 10 December, orders were issued by 6.Panzer-Armee to the corps under its command:

'On O-Tag at 6.00 am, I.SS-Panzerkorps will break through the enemy positions in the sector Hollerath-Krewinkel with its infantry divisions. It will then thrust to beyond the Meuse in the sector Liège-Huy with 12.SS-Panzer-Division on the right and 1.SS-Panzer-Division on the left.

'Bridges on the Meuse will be taken in undamaged condition by ruthless and rapid penetration. This will be accomplished by specially

organised forward detachments, under the command of suitable officers.'

The attack sector assigned to 6.Panzer-Armee was manifestly unsuitable for a rapid breakthrough. The commander of the vanguard I.SS-Panzerkorps, SS-Gruppenführer Hermann Priess, explained after the war that 'the area assigned to the corps for attack was unfavourable. It was broken and heavily wooded. At this time of the year and in the prevailing weather conditions, the area was barely negotiable. Few roads were available, and in the sector that we had to negotiate at the beginning of our attack, these were single-track, in many cases woodland and field tracks. It had to be taken into account that they would be axle-deep in mud, and that the type of vehicle usually at our disposal for such purposes could be made to negotiate it only with difficulty.'

A corps request to transfer the attack further to the south where better roads were available was not approved by the Army, and I.SS-Panzerkorps had to comply with the orders. After careful examination of the existing roads and evaluation of the terrain, five 'Rollbahn' were designated for the two Panzer divisions of the corps in the first wave; the three on the right, reaching the Meuse in the Liège sector, were assigned to 12.SS-Panzer-Division, and the two on the left, reaching the Meuse between

**SS-Ostubaf. Joachim Peiper, commander of SS-Panzer-Regiment 1, photographed during an award ceremony in autumn 1944. He wears black SS-Panzer vehicle uniform and a black shirt; note his Knight's Cross with Oakleaves at the throat, the 'LAH' cyphers on his shoulderstraps of rank, and the 'Adolf Hitler' cufftitle.**

Huy and Ombret-Rawsa, to 1.SS-Panzer-Division. Despite the fact that the orders specified that Liège was to be bypassed to the south, the Army staff accepted the idea of using some routes by-passing the town to the north: in addition to the fact that there were ideal bridging sites there, with flat banks allowing easy access to the river, the narrowness of the Army sector left them with no choice. As a counter-attack by the three American divisions assumed to be in the Elsenborn area had to be considered a possibility, it was hoped to avoid the Panzer divisions becoming embroiled in this potential battle area by keeping their lines of advance away from the northern shoulder; this would also ease the traffic problem, as they would be less likely to interfere with the movement of the infantry divisions responsible for the northern flank. That placed the main armoured strength and the Schwerpunkt—the point of main effort—on 'Roll-bahn C' and 'D'. Of the five lines of advance, except for 'Rollbahn C' which kept at least to secondary roads, the rest all had several stretches of forest trails or cross-country tracks, particularly over the vital first 20 kilometres.

In the first wave the 'specially organised

**The planned axes of advance, coded 'Rollbahn A' to 'E'.**

detachments, under the command of suitable officers' which were assembled within both of I.SS-Panzerkorps' Panzer divisions were two battle groups, each formed around their division's Panzer regiment and under the command of their respective regimental commanders. Kampfgruppe Kühlmann of the 12.SS-Panzer-Division was led by SS-Sturmbannführer Herbert Kühlmann; and Kampfgruppe Peiper of the 1.SS-Panzer-Division by SS-Obersturmbannführer Joachim Peiper. These battle groups were to make the key spearhead thrusts, forging a path to the Meuse on the inner, unexposed flanks of the divisions.

Each of the division's reconnaissance battalions was to be reinforced, and these groups—Kampfgruppe Bremer of the 12.SS-Panzer-Division, led by SS-Sturmbannführer Gerhard Bremer, and Kampfgruppe Knittel of the 1.SS-Panzer-Division, led by SS-Sturmbannführer Gustav Knittel—were to probe ahead along side roads as an advance detachment, avoiding giving battle as far as possible, to capture and hold a bridge or bridges across the river. The divisions' main elements were deployed as follows (though Rudolf Lehmann, the I.SS-Panzerkorps' chief-of-staff, has given a slightly different breakdown):

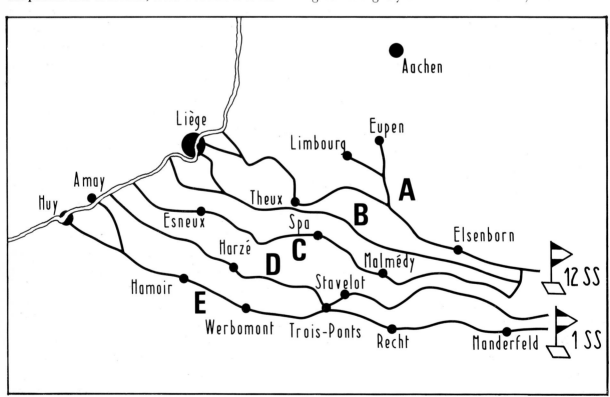

*Rollbahn A*

On the right, to be used by I.Btl., SS-Pz.Gren.Rgt. 25, which was to link with the paratroops of Operation 'Stösser' holding the crossroads in the forest near Mont Rigi.

*Rollbahn B*

Designated for Kampfgruppe Müller, under the command of SS-Sturmbannführer Siegfried Müller, comprising: SS-Pz.Gren.Rgt.25 (minus its I.Btl. on Rollbahn A), SS-Pz.Jg.Abt.12, an artillery battalion, and an engineer company.

*Rollbahn C*

The first group to move forward along this route was to be Kampfgruppe Kühlmann, comprising: SS-Pz.Rgt.12, including s.Pz.Jg.Abt.560, a Panzergrenadier battalion, a self-propelled artillery battalion, and an engineer company.

The second was Kampfgruppe Bremer, the reinforced divisional reconnaissance battalion, SS-Pz.Aufkl.Abt.12.

The third was Kampfgruppe Krause, commanded by SS-Obersturmbannführer Bernhard Krause, comprising: SS-Pz.Gren.Rgt.26 (minus its III. Btl. included in Kampfgruppe Kühlmann), an artillery battalion and a rocket launcher battalion, and the bulk of the division's Flak and engineer units.

The 12.SS-Panzer-Division staff were also to use this route.

*Rollbahn D*

First to move forward on this route was to be Kampfgruppe Peiper.

Second, Kampfgruppe Sandig led by SS-Obersturmbannführer Rudolf Sandig, comprising: SS-Pz.Gren.Rgt.2 (minus its III.Btl. included in Kampfgruppe Peiper), an artillery battalion, and the bulk of 1.SS-Panzer-Division's Flak and engineer units.

The staff of both 1.SS-Panzer-Division and I.SS-Panzerkorps were to use this route.

*Rollbahn E*

First, Kampfgruppe Hansen, under SS-Standartenführer Max Hansen, comprising: SS-Pz.Gren.Rgt.1, SS-Pz.Jg.Abt.1, an artillery battalion and an engineer company.

Second, Kamfpgruppe Knittel, the reinforced divisional reconnaissance battalion, SS-Pz.Aufkl. Abt.1.

On 14 December the commander of 1.SS-Panzer-Division, SS-Oberführer Wilhelm Mohnke, called a briefing at divisional headquarters in Tondorf for his regimental commanders, attended by Hansen, Sandig, Peiper and Knittel. Skorzeny was there too with some of his officers, as Kampfgruppe X of Panzerbrigade 150 was to operate in conjunction with Peiper's forces. Mohnke announced what was about to happen, and left them in no doubt as to the all-important rôle of the divisional units placed under their command, particularly of those forming the spearhead thrust to be made by Kampfgruppe Peiper.

Peiper, although he knew nothing of the offensive prior to this briefing, had deduced that something was in the air when he had been approached three days beforehand by the 6.Panzer-Armee chief-of-staff, SS-Brigadeführer Fritz Krämer, who asked him, 'what I thought about the possibility of an attack in the Eifel region and how much time it would take a Panzer regiment to proceed 80km in one night. Feeling that it was not a good idea to decide the answer to such a question merely by looking at a map, I made a test run of 80km with a Panther myself, driving down the route Euskirchen-Münstereifel-Blankenheim. I replied that if I had a free road to myself, I could make 80km in one night; of course, with an entire division, that was a different question.'

Kampfgruppe Peiper was made up of I.Abteilung of SS-Pz.Rgt.1, comprising 1. and 2.Kompanies with Panthers and 6. and 7.Kompanies with Panzer IVs; 9.Kompanie (engineers); and 10.Kompanie (anti-aircraft) with self-propelled Wirbelwinds. To compensate for the missing II.Abteilung of the Panzer regiment, schwere SS-Panzer-Abteilung 501 was attached with Tiger IIs; III.Btl. (infantry) and 13.(IG) Kompanie (self-propelled infantry guns) of SS-Pz. Gren.Rgt.2; II.Abteilung of SS-Pz.Art. Rgt.1; 3.Kompanie of SS-Pz.Pi.Btl.1 (engineers); and Flaksturm-Abteilung 84, a Luftwaffe Flak unit, formerly corps troops.

There has been a widespread tendency to grossly

exaggerate the strength of Kampfgruppe Peiper, which, had the Panzer regiment been up to full strength at mid-1944 levels, would have possessed at the most 180 tanks. At the time of the offensive the total cannot have been more than about 100 and was probably nearer 90: roughly equal numbers of 35 Panthers and Panzer IVs, and about 20 Tiger IIs.

Kampfgruppe Peiper (and more generally, any Panzer division) has often been claimed—particularly in books or magazines for modellers—to operate every type of Panzer, and particularly the 'star' tanks such as Tigers, Jagdtigers or Jagdpanthers. . . Even if pragmatic measures had been taken by the Wehrmacht in late 1944 to make up for the losses and difficulties, the distribution of Panzers at least kept to some basic rules to which we find only few exceptions.

**Three frames from a film showing Tiger II tanks of schwere SS-Pz-Abt. 501 moving through Tondorf on their way to Kampfgruppe Peiper's assembly area on the eve of the offensive. Their so-called 'ambush' colourschemes are clearly visible.**

The Panzer divisions were already under strength when the Allies invaded France in June 1944, and their situation had not improved since. As a result of attrition in the front lines, and the disruption caused by Allied bombing, the nominal establishment of 22 tanks per company for a 1944 Panzer regiment had fallen to 17; and by November 1944 to 14. Each Panzer-Regiment should have had two battalions, one equipped with Panzer IVs and the other with Panthers. This could not be universally achieved; some regiments had one battalion equipped partly, or even entirely, with StuGs in default of battle tanks. According to the summary *Auffrischung der Panzer Division im Westen*, in late November 1944 the 2.SS-Panzer-Division, 9.SS-Panzer-Division, 2.Panzer-Division and the 11.Panzer-Division each had two companies of StuGs instead of Panzer IVs; and 9.Panzer-Division and 116.Panzer-Division had no Panzer IV at all, but three companies of StuGs instead.

Other Panzer regiments had organised one battalion with an assortment of both types of

Panzer—two companies of Panzer IVs and two of Panthers—and a Panzer or Panzerjäger unit had been attached temporarily to the division to stand in for the second battalion. In November 1944 1.SS-Panzer-Division had received in this manner schwere SS-Panzer-Abteilung 501 (with Tiger IIs); 12.SS-Panzer-Division, schwere Panzer-Jäger-Abteilung 560 (Jagdpanthers and StuGs); 21.Panzer-Division, Sturm-Geschütz-Brigade 243 (StuGs); the Panzer-Lehr-Division, schwere Panzer-Jäger-Abteilung 559 (Jagdpanthers and StuGs); and 10.SS-Panzer-Division, schwere Panzer-Jäger-Abteilung 655 (Jagdpanthers and StuGs).

Peiper commented in a US Army interview after the war: 'I was supposed to have one battalion of Panthers in addition to one of Panzer IVs, and not having enough tanks I had to organise one battalion with a mixture of two companies of Panzer IVs and two of Panthers. To compensate for the shortage of tanks, my regiment was further reinforced with a battalion of Tigers which had been formerly corps troops. Therefore the regiment finally consisted of one battalion of mixed Panzer IVs and Panthers and one of Tigers.'

Among them is Tiger '222', which was also photographed later at Deidenberg and Kaiserbarracke, and which would end its career near the Stavelot bridge on 19 December.

Another 'star' of the Tondorf sequence was Tiger '008' of the battalion staff; note the letter 'G' painted on the glacis. Immobilised by mechanical trouble, it would later be the last Panzer still fighting on the northern bank of the Amblève between Stavelot and Trois-Ponts; and would be set on fire there by its crew on 25 December.

The Panzer divisions did have Jagdpanzer IVs, as this vehicle equipped two companies of the Panzer division's Panzer-Jäger-Abteilung, the third company being equipped with towed anti-tank guns.

The StuGs were a common sight; besides filling holes in the Panzer regiments and Panzerjäger battalions as described above, they equipped the Sturm-Geschütz-Brigade and most of the Sturm-Geschütz-Kompanie in the infantry divisions (one such company with each division). The Jagdpanzer 38(t) was not allocated to the Panzer divisions, but equipped the Sturm-Geschütz-Kompanie of those infantry divisions which had not received the StuGs.

The SdKfz 186 'Jagdtiger' was a rare sight in December 1944, as it had only been issued to schwere Panzer-Jäger-Abteilung 653, which had been prepared for action as corps troops within 'Wacht am Rhein' but which was eventually engaged within Operation 'Nordwind'.

The situation was equally simple for the self-propelled artillery guns: within the Panzer divisions, the SdKfz 138/1 'Bison' equipped the 13.(IG) Kompanie of the Panzergrenadier-Regiment; the SdKfz 124 'Wespe' and the SdKfz 165 'Hummel' equipped two or three batteries of the Panzer-Artillerie-Regiment. The SdKfz 166 'Brummbär' had been issued only to three independent Sturmpanzer-Abteilung, and the 'Sturmtiger' to three independent Sturmmörser-Kompanie.

## 15 December

Peiper called the commanders of the various units attached to the Kampfgruppe to his headquarters in a forester's hut near Blankenheim, and briefed them on the Kampfgruppe's operational rôle and how its forces were to be organised. The two Panzer IV companies would be at the front, followed by the two Panther companies, with the half-tracks transporting the Panzergrenadiers dispersed among them. These combat elements were to be followed by artillery and engineer units, while schwere SS-Panzer-Abteilung 501 would bring up the rear with its powerful Tiger IIs: Peiper regarded these bulky tanks as offering little advantage in the swift battles of movement—which he was being called upon to conduct. SS-Obersturmbannführer Willi Hardieck,

All crews were alert to the danger which constantly threatened them from a sky dominated by Allied tactical aircraft; an aircraft sentry was always on watch in every vehicle, and this photo shows the AA MG mount on Tiger '003'.

commander of the Panzerbrigade 150 battle group operating with 1.SS-Panzer-Division, was present at this briefing.

## 16 December

When the artillery barrage opened at 5.00 am, Peiper was at the command post of 12.Volks-Grenadier-Division with its commander, General-major Gerhardt Engel, watching the progress of the grenadiers to assess the right moment to launch his Kampfgruppe. From the messages coming in, it quickly became evident that the grenadiers were not moving as expected, and Peiper left, somewhat dispointed, at 2.00 pm.

Meanwhile the Kampfgruppe had started moving out of its assembly area in the Blankenheim forest, to an area immediately behind the front. Near Scheid it became entangled in a mass of vehicles belonging to 1.SS-Panzer-Division, 12.Volks-Grenadier-Division and 3.Fallschirm-Jäger-Division: the road from Scheid to Losheim was one massive traffic jam, as the bridge over a railway cutting about 2 km east of Losheimer-graben had been blown up by the Germans in their retreat and had not been rebuilt. When Peiper joined his units at 2.30 pm he was so angered by the whole mess that he ordered his own column to move ruthlessly ahead, shouldering off the road anything that got in its way. In this way the Kampfgruppe soon succeeded in reaching the railway cutting, where Peiper himself spent several hours attempting to restore some order. Bypassing the site of the bridge a few tens of metres to the right, his column moved down the side of the cutting at a point where it was less steep, across the tracks, and up the other side to regain the road.

By late evening the Kampfgruppe was back on the main road near Losheim, and by 10.00 pm the leading elements of s.SS-Pz.Abt.501 had caught up and joined the others. At Losheim Peiper learned from the division that F.J.Rgt.9 of 3.Fallschirm-Jäger-Division had achieved a breakthrough south of the village and was now fighting west of Lanzerath. He ordered his Kampfgruppe to move at once to take advantage of the breach, the grenadiers of SS-Hauptsturmführer Georg Preuss's 10.Kompanie leading the way; but problems arose in finding a safe way south of Losheim, because of

the large number of mines which had been sown there. When Peiper heard that the mine detectors were somewhere back in the column, he ordered the units to progress regardless: he lost some vehicles in the process but saved precious hours. Just before midnight the vanguards reached Lanzerath, and Peiper met Oberst i.G. von Hoffman, commanding F.J.Rgt.9 in the village café. The two men became involved in a heated argument, as Peiper was none too happy about what he considered to be Hoffmann's overcautious attitude in waiting for artillery support. I.SS-Panzerkorps then ordered that the first battalion of F.J.Rgt.9 be subordinated temporarily to Kampfgruppe Peiper.

## 17 December

Kampfgruppe Peiper, with two Panthers leading the column followed by a mixture of half-tracks, Panthers and Panzer IVs, had left Lanzerath on 'Rollbahn D' between midnight and 1.00 am. The night was very dark, and the vehicles moved ahead under black-out conditions along minor roads

**A common sight on the first day of the offensive: a road jammed with traffic. At right, SS-Oberführer Wilhelm Mohnke, commander of 1.SS-Pz-Div., stands up in his Kubelwagen in frustration.**

through the woods, with paratroopers holding white handkerchiefs walking beside each vehicle to guide the drivers. At about 5.00 am the column passed through Buchholtz. The village had been taken earlier by a probing force of F.J.Rgt.9; but an American radio operator had escaped the search and, hidden in the cellar of the former battalion HQ, he reported back on the strength of the German column. He counted 30 tanks and 28 half-tracks. . .

At around 6.00 am, just before daybreak, the column entered Honsfeld. Calmly joining the stream of American traffic that had trundled through that night, the Kampfgruppe's leading Panthers rolled down the village streets. The American troops in Honsfeld—elements of the 99th Infantry Div. and men of the 14th Cavalry Group—were taken by surprise, and offered little resistance; most became caught up in a desperate attempt to get out of the village. Those who escaped moved back to Hepscheid or as far back as Born and Medell. Peiper later referred to the amount of booty

captured in the village: some 15 anti-tank guns, 80 trucks, and 50 reconnaissance vehicles, including half-tracks. At dawn the paratroopers returned to the command of F.J.Rgt.9, but some of them, amounting to about a company, were to ride on the Panzers further west, until Stavelot and Stoumont.

A squadron of American fighter-bombers circled overhead and attacked the column, which had resumed its move westwards. The 'Wirbelwind' opened up on them and aircraft were brought down, but not before one or two 'Wirbelwind' had been destroyed, together with a few other vehicles damaged.

At the outskirts of Honsfeld, Peiper decided to deviate a little from 'Rollbahn D'. The condition of the roads west of Honsfeld was atrocious, and as he was already running low on fuel he decided to try to refuel at an American fuel dump at Büllingen. The

**German engineers have just completed this J-type bridge across the railway cutting near Losheim; a convoy of 1.SS-Pz-Div. drive across, guarded by a Luftwaffe AA crew and their 20mm Flak 38 mount.**

village was actually on 'Rollbahn C', assigned to 12.SS-Panzer-Division, but judging by the sounds of fighting to his right and from the rear, Peiper concluded that the division was still far behind. At around 8.00 am the grenadiers entered Büllingen without opposition except for a skirmish south of the village, when troops defending a small grass airstrip near Morschneck put up some resistance. The field was soon overrun, 12 light aircraft being destroyed in the process. Peiper found the depot he was looking for, and 50 prisoners were soon set to work filling the tanks of his vehicles with some of the 50,000 gallons of fuel seized.

At 9.30 am American batteries emplaced near Bütgenbach laid down a heavy barrage on the village. Small reconnaissance probes were sent northwards, but these were checked and turned back, and at around 10.00 am the advance elements

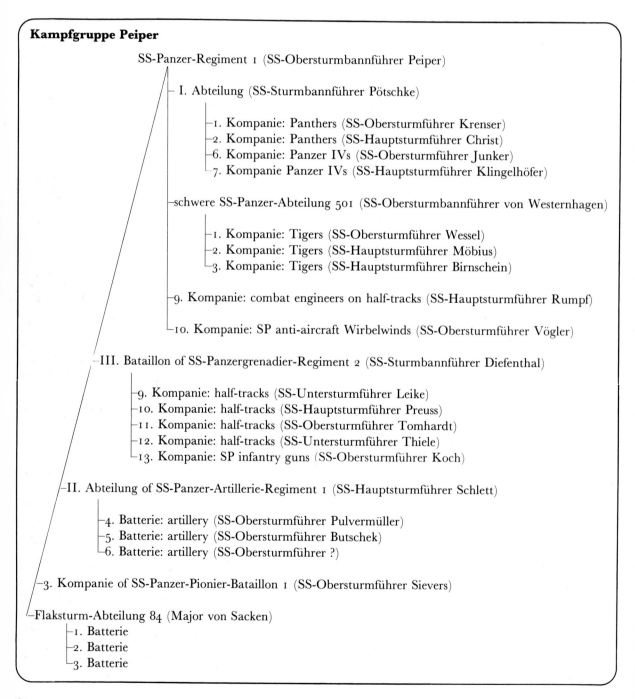

**Kampfgruppe Peiper**

SS-Panzer-Regiment 1 (SS-Obersturmbannführer Peiper)

– I. Abteilung (SS-Sturmbannführer Pötschke)

  –1. Kompanie: Panthers (SS-Obersturmführer Krenser)
  –2. Kompanie: Panthers (SS-Hauptsturmführer Christ)
  –6. Kompanie: Panzer IVs (SS-Obersturmführer Junker)
  –7. Kompanie Panzer IVs (SS-Hauptsturmführer Klingelhöfer)

–schwere SS-Panzer-Abteilung 501 (SS-Obersturmbannführer von Westernhagen)

  –1. Kompanie: Tigers (SS-Obersturmführer Wessel)
  –2. Kompanie: Tigers (SS-Hauptsturmführer Möbius)
  –3. Kompanie: Tigers (SS-Hauptsturmführer Birnschein)

–9. Kompanie: combat engineers on half-tracks (SS-Hauptsturmführer Rumpf)

–10. Kompanie: SP anti-aircraft Wirbelwinds (SS-Obersturmführer Vögler)

–III. Bataillon of SS-Panzergrenadier-Regiment 2 (SS-Sturmbannführer Diefenthal)

  –9. Kompanie: half-tracks (SS-Untersturmführer Leike)
  –10. Kompanie: half-tracks (SS-Hauptsturmführer Preuss)
  –11. Kompanie: half-tracks (SS-Obersturmführer Tomhardt)
  –12. Kompanie: half-tracks (SS-Untersturmführer Thiele)
  –13. Kompanie: SP infantry guns (SS-Obersturmführer Koch)

–II. Abteilung of SS-Panzer-Artillerie-Regiment 1 (SS-Hauptsturmführer Schlett)

  –4. Batterie: artillery (SS-Obersturmführer Pulvermüller)
  –5. Batterie: artillery (SS-Obersturmführer Butschek)
  –6. Batterie: artillery (SS-Obersturmführer ?)

–3. Kompanie of SS-Panzer-Pionier-Bataillon 1 (SS-Obersturmführer Sievers)

–Flaksturm-Abteilung 84 (Major von Sacken)
  –1. Batterie
  –2. Batterie
  –3. Batterie

left Büllingen. To the astonishment of the few American troops north of the village, they moved south-west towards Möderscheid instead of north towards Elsenborn. Not for the last time during the battle, strict adherence to strategic plans was to preclude considerable tactical success; but Peiper was intent on pressing forward along his assigned 'Rollbahn D', west towards Ligneuville and Stavelot. He had learned from an officer taken prisoner in Honsfeld that the 49th AAA Bde. had its headquarters in Ligneuville, and the idea of capturing an entire headquarters numbering over 400 men had spurred him on! All that slowed down the Kampfgruppe now was the state of the roads: narrow, muddy, and in some places little more than tracks. Brushing aside a handful of American troops at Möderscheid, the Kampfgruppe proceeded to Schoppen, Ondenval and on to Thirimont, which the vanguards reached at midday. The column swung north towards the hard-surfaced N32, and across the field to its left the N23 came suddenly into view.

The US 285th Field Artillery Observation Bn. was stationed near the 7th Armored Div. at Heerlem; and three serials of Bty. B—some 140 men and 30 vehicles—had been assigned to accompany the armoured division south. On the morning of 17 December the little convoy reached Malmédy; and although Capt. Roger L. Mills, the officer in charge of the column, was warned that German tanks were on the move somewhere to the east, he decided to take the risk, fearing that if they were diverted they might never get back in line. The little convoy had then taken the N32 in the direction of Baugnez. As the leading jeep approached the crossroads, Pte.

**The vanguard of 1.SS-Pz-Div. took hundreds of prisoners on the first days of the offensive; this young Waffen-SS Panzer man poses with a seemingly endless column. He wears black Panzer trousers with a jacket cut in Panzer style but from SS camouflage material, and displays his SS sleeve eagle and the Iron Cross 1st Class. The field service cap also appears to be of camouflage cloth.**

Tiger '222' again, here at Deidenberg on 18 December, speeding along 'Rollbahn E' with a load of paratroopers from FJR 9 clinging to the turret.

Homer Ford, the MP on duty, waved them on to the correct road. Suddenly, there came the sound of gunfire and Bty. B, whose leading vehicles had just reached the crossroads, came under fire.

Kampfgruppe Peiper, moving north from Thirimont, had reached the main road near Baugnez, and attacked the American convoy. From the moment the Panzers opened fire total confusion descended over the American column; vehicles were abandoned in panic and left standing where they were, some of them burning. Some of the men immediately threw away their weapons and ran towards the crossroads with their hands up. A few sought cover in the ditches on either side of the road and put up some resistance, while others tried to reach the edge of the nearby woods. The situation was hopeless, and Lt. Virgil T. Lary gave the word to stop firing and stood up to lead the surrender. The Germans searched the surrendering Americans, and then herded them into an open field next

to the crossroads. They were made to line up in eight rows, approximately 150 men all told. On the road the German column moved off towards Ligneuville, leaving the prisoners under light guard by the side of the road. Some of the captured transports had been included in the convoy, their former American drivers having 'volunteered' to drive them down to Ligneuville. Some time later, after 2.00 pm, shots rang out again, followed immediately by machine gun fire, which left most of the prisoners lying dead or wounded. After the firing stopped more single shots rang out, as those who still showed signs of life were finished off by some grenadiers who moved among the bodies. Quite a number of the Americans were still alive, feigning death; co-ordinating their timing in whispers, they suddenly rose to their feet and ran towards the woods to the north.

So many conflicting accounts have been written about this incident that it is very difficult today to establish precisely what happened at Baugnez crossroads on 17 December, 1944. The story produced by the prosecution at the post-war trial held at Dachau, describing an ordered and carefully prepared massacre, is far from convincing. Many details then accepted as true have since proved to be wrong. Among these is the position of the convoy, described as having passed the crossroads when it was stopped: pictures clearly show that at least a major part of it had been stopped before turning the crossroads. The misconduct of the prosecution team—later accused of having employed every means from confessions signed under duress, to fabricated evidence, mock trials, executions and beatings—casts some doubt upon the 'evidence' which they produced.

Another theory tries to explain that the massacre resulted from a tragic mistake when the main body of the Kampfgruppe came on the scene: mistaking the men standing in the field for combatants, the grenadiers opened fire as they approached. The range at which the firing took place, and the testimony of survivors who stated that the fire came from stationary vehicles rather than from tanks driving into battle, rule out this theory as well.

The 'Malmédy Massacre' was a genuine battle incident, possibly starting when some prisoners took the opportunity to make a break. For this or for another reason, a German fired a shot; whereupon panic broke out on both sides, the grenadiers opening up with machine guns. It then became a deliberate violation of the 'laws and usages of war', a war crime, as some of the grenadiers lost control of themselves and fired to kill, a handful of them even walking among the fallen bodies to give the *coup de grâce* to any Americans who still showed signs of life. Men of the same unit committed another war crime at Ligneuville, killing eight American prisoners; and behaved very violently towards civilians in the Stavelot area, killing tens of them without apparent reason. On the other hand, the same men took hundreds of American prisoners at Honsfeld, Cheneux and Stoumont without unnecessary

**Although not taken at Baugnez, this picture does give a good idea of the scene there on the morning of 17 December; PzKpfw IVs of 1.SS-Pz-Div., their crews taking some fresh air outside, clatter past several hundred American prisoners.**

violence, and were generally correct in their behaviour towards civilians. This somewhat contradictory behaviour may be explained by the suggestion that the less-experienced soldiers, possibly the youngest, lost control when faced with the tension and reality of battle.

The killing of men who had surrendered was a crime common to all the combatant armies in the Second World War; and there are several instances of retribution killings of captured grenadiers during the Battle of the Bulge, especially after the widespread publicity given by the US Army to the Baugnez incident to stiffen the Americans' resolve at a critical time. Paradoxically, though orders to kill prisoners could not be found in German files during the prosecution's preparation for the Dachau trial, such orders *were* issued by some American units, which fell victim to their own propaganda.

When the Panzers entered Ligneuville the commander of the 49th AAA Bde., Gen. Edwards J. Timberlake, and his staff had been gone for not more than ten minutes. At the southern edge of the village the leading tanks brushed with the rear elements of CCR, 7th Armored Div. moving out *en route* to Saint-Vith; but the main opposition came from some Shermans of the 9th Armored Div's. CCB, also moving south to join their unit at Saint-Vith. Charging at speed towards the Amblève bridge, the lead Panther was hit by a shell from a concealed Sherman and started to burn. The adjutant of I.Abteilung, SS-Untersturmführer Arndt Fisher, was riding in this Panther, and escaped from the burning vehicle with burns. In an SPW some distance behind, Peiper saw the Sherman's turret traversing towards his own vehicle; his driver hurriedly pulled back behind a house but another SPW was hit. Peiper jumped out and, taking a Panzerfaust, he began to stalk the troublesome tank; but before he could get within range it was hit by a Panzer and erupted in flames. The Kampfgruppe had lost a Panther and two other armoured vehicles; the Americans two

**This photo, taken at Kaiserbarracke, has appeared many times captioned as showing Peiper himself, but this is inaccurate. These men are actually NCOs of SS-Pz-Aufklärungs-Abt. 1, photographed at a spot which Peiper himself did not pass on 17 December: see commentary to Plate D2 for further details.**

Shermans, an M-10 tank destroyer and some men taken prisoner.

After a two-hour halt in Ligneuville to re-organise, the race westwards continued, and the column moved unopposed through the villages of Pont and Beaumont. Peiper was not at the front at this stage, as he was conferring in Ligneuville with his divisional commander, SS-Oberführer Wilhelm Mohnke.

At 7.30 pm the leading Panzers approached Stavelot, grinding slowly down the hill in darkness. Men of the US 291st Engineer Combat Bn. had established a roadblock at a bend of the road, with a rock face on one side and a steep drop on the other. As the Panzers approached one of the Americans shouted at them to halt. The grenadiers riding on the Panzers immediately opened fire, whereupon the engineers answered with bazookas. In total darkness, the Panzers retreated a few yards up the hill and the Americans moved back down towards Stavelot, leaving mines in place across the road. The Kampfgruppe's advance had temporarily stopped.

Tiger '222' again, in perhaps its best-known portrait: still with its load of Fallschirmjäger, it has now reached Kaiser-barracke, and rushes north towards Ligneuville. The tank commander, just visible behind the right-hand para, was SS-Unterscharführer Kurt Sova.

## 18 December

At 6.30 am Peiper, back with the vanguards, opened his attack with a preliminary artillery barrage which echoed in the Amblève valley until it got light enough to see at around 8.00 am. The Panzers had started rolling down the hill when shells from a 76mm gun, placed outside Stavelot on the Malmédy road by a unit of the 825th TD Bn., struck the column. The Kampfgruppe pushed down and reached the bottom of the valley; approaching the still-intact bridge, they man-oeuvred briefly before slowly driving across. Nothing happened: although the bridge was wired ready to be blown, something had gone wrong, either because of the haste and confusion among the American engineers, or because a German 'special' team had worked on it.

When the Panzers debouched from the bridge to drive up the Chatelet road they came under machine gun fire from the streets to the right, and dead ahead they encountered another 76mm gun at the main road junction in the market place. Taking a side street to bypass the gun, they climbed the steep Rue Haut-Rivage and managed to reach the main street to Trois-Ponts. When the American gunners saw that the Germans had passed them they spiked the gun with a grenade down the barrel and withdrew, leaving the way open for the Kampfgruppe to use the better Rue du Chatelet. The grenadiers did not waste time in mopping up resistance in the town; by 10.00 am the Kampfgruppe was beginning to leave Stavelot for Trois-Ponts, but the Germans only really controlled those parts of it through which they were advancing.

Maj. Paul J. Solis, the commander of the 526th Armored Infantry Bn. which had arrived at Stavelot the night before Peiper, ordered his troops to withdraw when the Panzers had got across the bridge, and most went out by the Malmédy road.

Solis took two rifle squads and made north to Francorchamps on a minor road. There was a huge fuel dump in the woods north of Stavelot, and Solis urged the detachment of Belgian troops guarding the dump to get on with setting fire to it, both to block the road and to deny the fuel to the Panzers. All this proved unnecessary, as Peiper did not even attempt to send a reconnaissance in that direction; but when element of the US 117th Regt. of the 30th Infantry Div., approaching Stavelot by this back road later that morning, ordered a halt to the burning, 145,000 US gallons of petrol had gone up in flames.

Having gained the north bank of the Amblève, Peiper faced his next crucial river crossing at Trois-Ponts; at this point 'Rollbahn D' and 'Rollbahn E' converged to cross the Salm and Amblève rivers. It seems that Peiper had already decided to leave his assigned 'Rollbahn D' and to follow the more passable 'Rollbahn E' through Werbomont and Hamoir towards Huy. To make certain of seizing the crucial Trois-Ponts bridges, Peiper had organised a two-pronged attack: as his Panzers were attacking down the hill into Stavelot to follow

These two 37mm Flak 36 AA guns, one mounted on a Daimler-Benz L4500A truck and the other on an SdKfz 6/2 half-track, were disabled near Lodometz by fighter-bombers shooting up the column of Kampfgruppe Peiper on 18 December.

The next three pictures are from an impressive sequence showing 2.Kompanie, SS-PzGren-Rgt.1 'attacking' near Poteau on the morning 18 December. In reality the pictures were posed, in front of numerous American vehicles abandoned on the road—all that remained of Task Force Mayes of the 14th Cavalry Group, which had been destroyed there. See also Plate J. This SS-Rottenführer armed with a StG 44 pretends to signal his men onwards.

'Rollbahn D' on the northern bank of the Amblève, a smaller force was moving through Wanne to threaten Trois-Ponts along 'Rollbahn E'.

The leading elements of the Kampfgruppe were sighted at about 10.45 am approaching Trois-Ponts, where they were challenged by a lone 76mm gun; a Panzer was hit and temporarily stopped, but the next opened fire on the gun, killing all four members of the crew. At 11.15 am the bridge over the Amblève was blown, blocking the Kampfgruppe on the northern bank of the river. The southern part of the pincer attack against Trois-Ponts was now ready on the heights overlooking the Salm River bridge. The Panzers had still to detour a long way along the road before they could reach the town, but the grenadiers poured down the wooded slope to the river below. At 1.00 pm, just as they reached the vicinity of the bridge, the American engineers blew it in their faces. Leaving only some troops on the southern bank of the Amblève, that part of the Kampfgruppe withdrew to Wanne and

Three SS-Schütze 'attack' across the road, the first armed with an MP 40, the second with a Kar 98 rifle and the third with a captured M1 carbine.

The same men—the three 'attackers' on the left—share out American cigarettes for a well-earned smoke with the much-photographed MG 42 gunner who also has a Belgian-made Browning 9mm High-Power in his hand, and a fighting knife tucked into the front of his smock.

then to Stavelot to join up again with the main body of the Kampfgruppe.

With the destruction of the Amblève bridge, Peiper had no option but to take the road north to La Gleize, the route of his originally designated 'Rollbahn D'. They met no opposition between Trois-Ponts and La Gleize, which was passed through at 1.00 pm, and advance units reported having captured a bridge across the Amblève at Cheneux; the American engineers had not been given orders to destroy it, and it left a loophole in their defences which Peiper exploited to the full. By 2.00 pm, as the head of the column had just crossed the bridge, American fighter-bombers appeared and attacked the columns. The 'Wirbelwinds' fought back, but the grenadiers had to take cover in the woods between the bridge and Cheneux, and the Kampfgruppe was not able to get going again until about 4.00 pm, when fog came down and hid it from the air. The aircraft had bombed and strafed the whole column from Lodometz near Stavelot to Cheneux, and the actual losses for Peiper were a

dozen vehicles, among them two Panthers; yet the most vital loss was two precious hours.

Peiper's intention was now to get on 'Rollbahn E' as soon as possible as this would take the Kampfgruppe all the way along the N23 to the Meuse at Huy. Only two bridges remained between him and his goal: one at Hamoir over the Ourthe, and another over the tiny Lienne at Neufmoulin. Towards 4.30 pm the leading vehicles reached the N23 just south of Froidville and turned right; up the road, an American engineer detail under Lt. Alvin Edelstein had just finished wiring the bridge, and it was blown as the Panzers approached. Peiper sent out probing forces to find another bridge solid enough for his tanks; but even though some SPWs actually reached the western bank of the Lienne, the bridges at Chauveheid and Moulin de Rahier were far too small to carry the weight of the 'armour' and he had to order his Kampfgruppe back up to La Gleize and 'Rollbahn D', leaving only a strong detachment at Cheneux to guard the bridge. At about 11.00 pm the Kampfgruppe halted in the woods between La Gleize and Stoumont.

To the rear, as Kampfgruppe Hansen could not make any progress along 'Rollbahn E', SS-Oberführer Mohnke ordered Kampfgruppe Knittel, which was waiting as a second echelon, to move north instead in support of Kampfgruppe Peiper. The unit proceeded via Pont and crossed the bridge at Stavelot at about 7.00 pm, behind elements of the force returning from Wanne to join with the main body. When Knittel reached Stavelot the situation was dangerous: since late afternoon US infantry of the 117th Regt. had been attacking the town, and at around 8.00 pm German vehicles were hit by tank destroyers in the market place, not 50m away from the main road to Trois-Ponts. Nevertheless, Knittel pressed on towards La Gleize not long after midnight; and that night, for all practical purposes, Stavelot could be considered as being back in American hands: Peiper was in great danger of being cut off.

## 19 December

After having rapidly assembled at first light, Peiper opened the attack on Stoumont at 9.00 am. To the left of the road was a drop which restricted the movement of the Panzers; but there were bare fields

1

Baugnez, 21 Dec. 1944:
1: Sturmgeschutz III Ausf. G, PzBde 150
2: SdKfz 250/5, PzBde 150

2

A

Kampfgruppe X, Malmédy, 21 Dec. 1944:
1, 2: PzKpfw V Ausf. G Panthers, PzBde 150

B

Ligneuville, 21 Dec. 1944:
Kampfgruppe X, PzBde 150

Oblt. Deier        SS-Hstuf. von Foelkersoam        'Special Guide'

VOLSTAD

C

1: SdKfz 250/7, SS-Pz-Aufkl-Abt 1
2: Schwimmwagen, SS-Pz-Aufkl-Abt 1

Kaiserbarracke, 18 Dec. 1944

D

1

Ligneuville, 18 Dec. 1944:
1: PzKpfw VI Ausf. B Tiger, s/SS-Pz-Abt 501
2: PzKpfw V Ausf. G Panther, SS-Pz-Rgt 1

2

E

La Gleize, 19 Dec. 1944:
1: PzKpfw IV Ausf. J, SS-Pz-Rgt 1

2: SdKfz 138/1, SS-PzGren-Rgt 2

F

Stoumont, 19 Dec. 1944:
1: PzKpfw V Ausf. G Panther, SS-Pz-Rgt 1
2: Wirbelwind, s/SS-Pz-Abt 501

1

2

G

1

La Gleize, 20 Dec. 1944:
1: PzKpfw VI Ausf. B Tiger, s/SS-Pz-Abt 501
2: SdKfz 251/3 Ausf. D, SS-PzGren-Rgt 2

2

H

1

Trois Ponts, 20-21 Dec. 1944:
1: Hummel, SS-Pz-Art-Rgt 1
2: Jagdpanzer IV/70, SS-PzJäg-Abt 1

2

I

Poteau, 18 Dec. 1944:
Men of 2 Kompanie, SS-PzGren-Rgt 1

1

2

3

J

Stoumont, 19 Dec. 1944:
Men of I/SS-Pz-Rgt 1

K

Stoumont, 19 Dec. 1944:
1: SS-Stubaf. Diefenthal
2: Oberjäger, FJR 9
3: SS-Schütze, III/SS-PzGren-Rgt 2

VOLSTAD

L

to the right of it, and the armour almost reached the village under cover of the early morning mist before they were spotted. The first tank to get into the village, a Panther, approached the church, but was knocked out by a 90mm anti-aircraft gun. The battle went on for nearly two hours, with the infantry attacking from the south while the Panzers advanced along the road, before the defence was finally breached and the village penetrated. The American defenders—the 3rd Bn., 119th Regt.—suffered some 250 casualties, and about 100 were taken prisoner.

Peiper wasted no time in despatching a probing force forward on the heels of the retreating Americans, and a few Panthers and half-tracks began to roll down the road towards the railway station behind the village. There, a company of the 740th Tank Bn., another from the 119th Infantry Regt. and two AAA batteries (the 110th and 143) had formed a strong roadblock awaiting the oncoming armour. At about 3.30 pm, just behind the last of the retreating US vehicles, a Panther suddenly appeared out of the fog almost on top of the American force. The Panther's overconfident crew were slow to react, and the Americans fired first. At that range the Panther stood no chance, and the shell ricochetted down from the gun mantlet, killing the driver instantly. Seconds later the Panther behind was also hit, and then a third. This action was the last attack westwards launched by Kampfgruppe Peiper.

It was the supply situation which ruled out further progress, and until supplies could be brought up all that could be done was to hold existing positions. 1.Kompanie of SS-Panzer-Regiment 1 was to hold the positions at Stoumont railway station and in the village, while 2.Kompanie was responsible for securing La Gleize against attack from the north and north-east; Flak-Sturm-

**Smoke drifts overhead as a Panther from 2.Kompanie, SS-Pz-Rgt.1 approaches Stoumont, passing an abandoned 76mm AT gun beside the La Gleize–Stoumont road: 19 December.**

In the outskirts of Stoumont the leading Panther has received a direct hit and starts to burn. Alert to the danger, the commander of the second tank, head exposed, cons his Panther forward. All these shots were actually taken in combat on 19 December.

Abteilung 84 was to hold the area around Cheneux to protect the Amblève crossing. Supporting the Panzers at Stoumont and reinforcing the troops at Cheneux were the grenadiers of III.Btl., SS-Panzergrenadier-Regiment 2. At about mid-day Peiper sent out a small patrol north from La Gleize. The half-tracks passed through Borgoumont and Cour but soon ran into the troops guarding a huge fuel storage depot; after a short skirmish, the patrol withdrew to La Gleize.

Since the afternoon Stoumont had been under constant artillery and mortar fire and, towards dusk, Peiper realised that his weak forces would be unable to maintain their hold on the 3 km between the village and the railway station. Reluctantly he ordered the troops to be withdrawn that evening, first to a hairpin bend along the road and finally, at 9.00 pm, to the edge of Stoumont. The Kampfgruppe command post was located in a house near the Froide-Cour château—the château itself being used as a clearing station and collecting point for prisoners.

By morning Priess had brought his I.SS-Panzerkorps headquarters forward at Holzheim and Mohnke his 1.SS-Panzer-Division headquarters to Wanne. Priess had understood that his best

chance of moving westwards lay with Peiper, and he had ordered the whole 1.SS-Panzer-Division to back up the Kampfgruppe's efforts. Kampfgruppe Sandig was ordered to take Stavelot, Kampfgruppe Hansen was to resume the advance along 'Rollbahn E' through Logbiermé and Wanne, and Kampfgruppe Knittel was sent back from La Gleize to Trois-Ponts to hold the vital supply road through Stavelot. Knittel's detachment made some progress on the heights west of Stavelot; but Hansen faced huge difficulties in assembling south of the river because of the atrocious state of the road. Sandig failed to cross the Amblève at Stavelot, and sent his II.Bataillon through Wanne towards Petit-Spai, where it was ordered to cross the bridge and join Peiper; elements did so on the next morning, and reached La Gleize around mid-day—the last grenadiers who would reach Kampfgruppe Peiper.

## 20 December

For I.SS-Panzerkorps the situation was at a turning point, as it struggled to support the adventurous Kampfgruppe Peiper which had achieved a deep penetration but was now blocked. Would it be resupplied and reinforced, or strangled?

The American decision to check and eliminate this dangerous breakthrough had resulted in the reorganisation of their strength in the area. In the middle of the previous afternoon the 119th Infantry Regt. and 740th Tank Bn., organised as Task Force

A knot of paratroopers set up a machine gun by a fence and hedge close to the burning Panther, from whose crew only SS-Rottenführer Heinz Hofmann escaped alive.

A photo of the same view, from further back; now a PzKpfw IV of 6.Kompanie, SS-Pz-Rgt.1 comes up, and a Panzer-Grenadier runs for better cover, as dark smoke from the burning Panther drifts upwards.

Same view, closer photograph: SS-Sturmbannführer Werner Pötschke, CO of I Abteilung, SS-Pz-Rgt.1, turns to pick up an abandoned Panzerfaust before returning to the battle. He wears a leather jacket and trousers over his uniform; his Knight's Cross, shoulder straps and collar patches can just be seen; see Plate K.

camouflaged convoy which had crossed Petit-Spai bridge and was trying to resupply Peiper at La Gleize. Moving south, the task force reached Trois-Ponts and turned left towards Stavelot; as they approached Petit-Spai the six leading Shermans were disabled by accurate fire from the Panzers and anti-tank guns emplaced on both sides of the river to cover the bridge, and the task force pulled back to the Biester area. Kampfgruppe Peiper was now completely cut off.

The ring was tightening on its southern flank as well when, late in the afternoon, the 504th Parachute Regt. attacked Cheneux. Peiper, well aware of the importance of this route for any future development, had reinforced the bridgehead with the elements of II.Btl., SS-Panzergrenadier-Regiment 2 as soon as they had reached La Gleize that morning. The paratroopers launched their assault across a bare field criss-crossed with barbed wire, and took heavy punishment. After three costly attempts they gained the first row of houses in the village; but part of Cheneux still remained in German hands when the fighting died away. On the western flank of Peiper's positions, Task Force Harrison had fought its way forward and attacked the Saint-Edouard sanatorium, a large building at the western edge of the village. Grim hand-to-hand fighting followed inside the building, but the grenadiers were outnumbered and by 8.00 pm the Americans were in control. Around midnight a fierce counter-attack put the grenadiers back in possession of 'Festung Sankt-Edouard', the Germans taking 30 prisoners in the process, and destroying five Shermans.

To the rear, the situation was getting worse and worse: Knittel had to disengage from the heights and pulled back towards Petit-Spai; Sandig launched another unsuccessful attack against Stavelot, and at about 5.00 am the bridge was blown by men of A Co., 105th Engineers Combat Battalion.

## 21 December

I.SS-Panzerkorps envisaged the possibility of Kampfgruppe Peiper having to break its way out of the impasse; but the idea of a withdrawal was rejected by 6.Panzer-Armee, and 1.SS-Panzer-Division was ordered to intensify its efforts to back the Kampfgruppe.

Harrison, were assigned to the operational control of the XVIII Airborne Corps; at the same time the corps took back its 82nd Airborne Div. and received part of the 3rd Armored Division. Task Force Harrison was to advance on Stoumont; the Airborne's 504th Parachute Regt. was engaged towards Cheneux and its 505th Parachute Regt. farther east towards Trois-Ponts, while CCB of the 3rd Armored assembled near Theux.

On the morning of 20 December, CCB launched three task forces south: Task Force Jordan moved from the Spa area towards Stoumont, Task Force McGeorge towards Borgoumont and La Gleize, and Task Force Lovelady from Francorchamps towards Coo. Task Force Jordan made little progress, as the column was confined to the road by the high banks on either side, and as it approached Stoumont a Panzer knocked out its two leading tanks. Similarly, Task Force McGeorge was stopped around mid-day when it came up against a roadblock south of Borgoumont. To the east, Task Force Lovelady was more successful: pushing south without opposition, it got on to the main N23 between La Gleize and Coo and took by surprise a

Around La Gleize, the Kampfgruppe was no longer in a position to counter the American initiatives: it found itself trapped, without adequate supplies, in a narrow pocket. The need to consolidate the lines became even more evident when a small American outfit ventured as far as the Stoumont-La Gleize road; the grenadiers had thrown them back and taken prisoners (including the commander of the 2nd Bn., 119th Regt., Maj. Hal D. McCown), but not before the Americans had blocked the road by blasting down trees.

At noon Peiper called together his senior commanders at his command post in the gatekeeper's lodge of the Froide-Cour château, and they decided to concentrate all the available forces around La Gleize and to try to keep open the bridge near Cheneux. The evacuation of the positions at Stoumont would leave the Froide-Cour château outside the defensive perimeter; inside the château were about 130 American prisoners and some 120 German and a number of American wounded. Before the line was pulled back, all the German walking wounded and all the prisoners were taken to La Gleize; about 80 German and all the American wounded remaining in the château under the care of a German medical surgeon and two American medical privates. The withdrawal from the Stoumont area and back across the Amblève from Cheneux to defensive positions immediately behind the bridge was carried out without incident. In Cheneux fierce house-to-house fighting persisted between the 504th paratroopers and the rearguard covering the contraction of the bridgehead.

The morning of 21 December saw the bulk of 1.SS-Panzer-Division massed on the heights between Trois-Ponts and Wanne. Heavy equipment began to move down the hill towards the Petit-Spai bridge, but the weight of the first heavy vehicle—a Jagdpanzer IV/70—brought the flimsy structure down around it. Engineers set about erecting a new bridge just above the collapsed one, and had just got a girder in position above the strong current when intensive artillery fire was laid on the site, bringing work to an end. Infantry could still cross over the wreckage, and elements of SS-Panzergrenadier-Regiment 1 crossed during the night and began to move north. A few kilometres to the south, the grenadiers made another effort against Trois-Ponts

A Panther commander urges some prisoners out of his path as he negotiates the narrow village street. Note the camouflage paint and foliage on the turret.

and renewed their attack along 'Rollbahn E' at noon. Two companies of the 505th Parachute Infantry which were established east of the Salm were forced into a desperate retreat, and the Salm bridge, which had been made usable to support the bridgehead east of the river, had to be blown for the second time in four days.

## 22 December

Although 9.SS-Panzer-Division had been committed on the left of 1.SS-Panzer-Division, and the efforts of I.SS-Panzerkorps were about to be reinforced by those of II.SS-Panzerkorps, the situation of Kampfgruppe Peiper was hopeless. American artillery had not let up all night; in the morning Task Force McGeorge and the 119th Regt. took the Froide-Cour area. Confused and fierce fighting took place for individual houses on the edges of La Gleize but, when the fighting subsided at the end of the afternoon, the grenadiers had succeeded in restoring their perimeter. Supplies of fuel and ammunition were practically exhausted, and no food had arrived since the first day of the attack. The Luftwaffe supply drop requested by I.SS-Panzerkorps was made at about 8.00 pm. Twenty aircraft were despatched for this attempt to resupply the Kampfgruppe; but many of the containers were released over Stoumont, parachuting straight into American hands, and Peiper estimated that only ten per cent of the supplies dropped actually reached his men. The amount of fuel was too small to have any effect, being just

Edging down the narrow street of Stoumont, a Panther is waved forward to support the grenadiers. Note heavy foliage camouflage, loose side skirt plate, and jerrycan slung on turret.

sufficient to keep the radio functioning and to get a few Panzers into firing positions. Again I.SS-Panzerkorps asked for permission for the Kampfgruppe to be allowed to fight its way out, but again 6.Panzer-Armee rejected the request, and the corps had to order 1.SS-Panzer-Division to increase its efforts to link up with Peiper.

In the Trois-Ponts area, Knittel's detachment had pulled back from the fighting for Stavelot, and with these reinforcements Kampfgruppe Hansen increased its efforts along the N33, being rewarded in the afternoon with the capture of Biester; part of Task Force Lovelady became cut off from its rear between Biester and Trois-Ponts. This was a short-lived success as the grenadiers were fighting without any heavy equipment or supporting armour and were unable to get any closer to La Gleize.

## 23 December
The village of La Gleize, the group of Wérimont farms and the hamlet of La Venne now comprised the only ground still occupied by the Kampfgruppe. During the afternoon the American artillery stepped up its bombardment even further, turning La Gleize into an inferno. From Froide-Cour, Task Force Jordan pushed for La Venne but was immediately stopped by a Panther and a Panzer IV hidden in the woods by La Venne crossroads. That morning the corps received a message from Peiper: 'Position considerably worsened. Meagre supplies of infantry ammunition left. Forced to yield Stoumont and Cheneux during the night. This is the last chance of breaking out'. The corps finally gave the order for men and vehicles to break out eastwards, an order which Peiper received at about 5.00 pm. He knew that this was now impossible as there was just not enough fuel left to fight their way out, and that all they could do was to slip away, leaving behind all their heavy equipment, the prisoners and the wounded. He called together his senior commanders at his command post in the cellar of a ruined house, and they worked out plans for evacuation that night.

The battle between Task Force Lovelady and Kampfgruppe Hansen, still trying to extend the bridgehead north of Trois-Ponts along the N33, raged all day, but at no time did the grenadiers succeed in breaking through.

**American prisoners from 3rd Bn., 119th Inf.Rgt. are marched away from a building in Stoumont by confident grenadiers of III/SS-PzGren-Rgt.2—few of whom could imagine how soon their rôles would be reversed.**

## 24 December

At about 2.00 am Peiper led what was left of his Kampfgruppe—less than 1,000 men, on foot southwards to La Venne. A small rearguard stayed behind at La Gleize to hold off the Americans and to try to destroy the armour and vehicles remaining in the village. The American prisoners and the German wounded had been left behind but, according to an agreement Peiper had proposed to his senior prisoner, Maj. McCown, the German wounded were to be set free after they had recovered in American hospitals in return for the American prisoners left in La Gleize. McCown had to remain with his captors, to be exchanged when the wounded were handed over. At La Venne officers checked the cellars to find guides to lead the withdrawal through the night: two local Belgians

'volunteered' and the column left the north bank of the Amblève for good.

Before dawn they were at Brume, where they joined a small vanguard group and proceeded northwards to the Coo valley with the intention of breaking through to Hansen's positions near Biester, but, with the Coo bridge down, the idea had to be called off. They remained hidden in nearby woods all day to avoid being spotted by low-flying American reconnaissance aircraft, and it was late afternoon before the column began moving southwards again. Just after dark the group crossed the N23 between Basse-Bodeux and Trois-Ponts; and shortly after midnight, near Bergeval, they ran into an American outpost. (During the ensuing skirmish Maj. McCown broke his parole and ran away.) They forded the icy waters of the Salm near Rochelinval, brushing again with American outposts, and came under machine gun fire. Climbing a steep hill east of Wanne, they linked up with the bulk of their division before dawn. Peiper reported to his corps commander at 10.00 am that morning; as Priess recalled after the war, the Kampfgruppe had made the break-out with about 800 men and had succeeded in arriving with 770. The group had been in combat, under the most severe conditions, for an uninterrupted period of a week, and they were so exhausted that it was only by the use of force that the men were prevented from falling asleep while on the march.

Meanwhile, as the Americans closed in on the morning of Christmas Eve, the Panther and Panzer IV near La Venne were finally silenced, and the village was entered against little opposition. The prisoners, about 170, were liberated and about 300 German wounded taken captive. Strewn throughout the village were tanks, guns and vehicles, of which few had been put out of action by the rearguards. About 25 Panzers and 50 SPWs were found in La Gleize itself, the total loss by the Kampfgruppe north of the Amblève amounting to about 45 tanks, the guns of two artillery batteries and more than 60 SPWs, not counting wheeled vehicles, flak wagons, heavy mortars, etc.

The Kampfgruppe had ceased to exist as a fighting force, and with it went Hansen's objective on the north bank of the Amblève. Late that afternoon, under renewed American pressure, Hansen ordered a general withdrawal to the south bank of the Amblève.

On Christmas Day the Tiger II still fighting on east of Petit-Spai near La Ferme Antoine was set alight, and the few grenadiers crossed over at Petit-Spai, the very last members of Kampfgruppe Peiper to leave the north bank of the Amblève.

Kampfgruppe Peiper was disbanded by divisional order, effective 26 December, which returned the individual units to their respective regiments. That day SS-Panzer-Regiment 1, which had lost nearly all its strength north of the Amblève, was transferred to the Saint-Vith area for rehabilitation, with orders to assemble a battalion with what had been left south of the river, to be ready for combat as soon as possible.

**A graveyard of SdKfz 251 half-tracks: the mounts of SS-PzGren-Rgt.2 lie scattered across the orchard below La Gleize. (La Gleize Museum)**

# The Plates

## A: Baugnez, 21 December:

### A1: Sturmgeschutz III Ausf.G, Panzerbrigade 150

The five Sturmgeschutze III allotted to Panzer-brigade 150 on 24 November were engaged east of Malmédy with Kampfgruppe Y on 21 December: these StuG 40 Ausf.G were largely unmodified except for the addition of new side skirts, which did little to disguise them. They were painted in American Olive Drab and displayed white stars on the front glacis, on both sides of the body and on the side skirts. The crew had been loaned to Panzerbrigade 150 by schwere Panzerjäger-Abteilung 655, and the men wore the usual field grey version of the black Panzer uniform. This particular StuG—which was marked '5△81△' 'C5', and was thus supposed to belong to C Co., 81st Tank Bn., 5th Armored Div.—was abandoned in a field by the road between Baugnez and Géromont.

### A2: SdKfz 250/5, Panzerbrigade 150

Originally, Skorzeny had planned to have two companies of recce armoured cars: 3.Kompanie with the Panthers of 1.Kompanie in the brigade's first battalion, and 10.Kompanie with the StuGs of 9.Kompanie in the second battalion. Just as he never obtained all the panthers and StuGs he hoped for, he never received all the recce vehicles he had planned to engage: he got very few genuine American armoured cars, and was allotted six Panzerspähwagen, armoured scout cars, on 24 November. We do not know precisely of which type these vehicles were, but it seems probable that they were eight-wheeled SdKfz 234 heavy armoured cars. Two recce units, one from 90.Panzergrenadier-Division and one from 2.Panzer-Division, had sent armoured car crews to 150.Panzerbrigade at Grafenwöhr. Some of these men actually brought their vehicles, and this may explain the presence, under Skorzeny's colours, of this somewhat elderly SdKfz 250/5. Although the type was manufactured right to the end, the early *alte* model had been replaced on the production lines by the *neu* body in 1943. A leichter Aufklärungspanzerwagen—light armoured recce car—the SdKfz 250/5 was equipped with a FuG12 radio set.

## B: Kampfgruppe X at Malmédy, 21 December:

### B1, B2: PzKpfw V Ausf.G Panthers, Panzerbrigade 150

The Panthers modified to represent M10s for Panzerbrigade 150 were painted in Olive Drab and displayed thickly ringed white stars on the front armoured plate and on both sides of the turret. Like all vehicles 'modified' for Panzerbrigade 150, the Panther/M10 displayed a yellow triangle at the rear. The Panther above, coded '5△10△' 'XY' 'B4' (see **B2** for style) was leading the attack in the direction of Malmédy when it hit a mine in front of the railway overpass to the south-west of the town. This marking was supposed to identify it as belonging to B Co., 10th Tank Bn., 5th Armored Div.; in fact it belonged to 4.Kompanie, Panzer-Regiment 11, 6.Panzer-Division. This tank, the mount of Leutnant Peter Mandt and his crew, was a platoon leader. The men were dressed as usual in their black Panzer uniform, but they had pulled on

The battle over, a Wirbelwind stands abandoned outside the hotly-contested 'Festung Sankt-Edouard' in Stoumont. (La Gleize Museum)

American jackets and trousers over it. The whole crew except Leutnant Mandt were killed.

The Panther coded '5△10△' 'XY' 'B7' (below) was the mount of Oberfeldwebel Bachmann and his crew; the star on the front was ringed but those on the turret were not. Ordered to lead an attack westwards in the direction of Stavelot on 21 December, the tank crossed over the Warche bridge and stopped by a house to wait for the other Panther, which seemed to be hesitant to follow. It was then struck by a bazooka round which penetrated the engine compartment, and the crew bailed out, running for the bridge and the southern bank of the river. Oberfeldwebel Bachmann, the driver Unteroffizier Stucken, the gunner Feldwebel Feit and the assistant gunner Gefreiter Salzmann were all killed when running for shelter; but the radio operator, Obergefreiter Karl Meinhardt, escaped unhurt, removing his American uniform and remaining hidden in a nearby house until captured on 27 December.

*C: Preparation for attack by Kampfgruppe X, Ligneuville, 21 December: SS-Hstuf. von Foelkersoam, Oblt.Deier, and 'Special Guide', Panzerbrigade 150*

The commander of Kampfgruppe X of Panzerbrigade 150, SS-Hauptsturmführer Adrian von Foelkersoam, discussed while at Ligneuville the

**The trial held by the Americans at Dachau, of German personnel held responsible for the massacre of US prisoners at Baugnez crossroads on 17 December. Objective consideration of the evidence accepted by the tribunal must lead the impartial reader to the conclusion that a hunger for revenge, however understandable, outweighed strict standards of military justice. The incident is discussed in detail in the text. Front row, left to right: Josef Dietrich, Fritz Krämer, Hermann Priess, Joachim Peiper. Second row: Manfred Coblenz, Arndt Fischer, Hans Gruhle, Hans Hennecke and Venoni Junker. Third row: Gustav Knittel (31), Werner Kühn (34), and Erich Münkemer (39).**

details of the attack about to start early on 21 December. With him were Oberleutnant Otto Deier, who was in command of the company of Panther/M10s assigned to Kampfgruppe X; and a 'special guide' dressed entirely as an American soldier. Oberleutnant Deier (**C2**) came from 4.Kompanie, Panzer-Regiment 11, 6.Panzer-Division, and was wearing his usual black Panzer uniform, with the black Einheitsmütze, common at this date, and the Panzer Battle Badge. He and his crews would don American clothing over their German uniforms just before going into action. SS-Hauptsturmführer von Foelkersoam (**C1**) wore the reversible winter over-uniform, the white side being innermost that day; and a field grey Einheitsmütze with the death's-head on the front of the crown and the eagle on the left side of the flap. Rank badges could be seen on the collar of the tunic he wore under his winter uniform and on the left sleeve of the latter; this green-on-black insignia was part of a ranking system devised early in 1943 for use on combat clothing without shoulder straps. He wore the Ritterkreuz which he had been awarded in 1942 when he was, as a member of a 'Brandenburg' unit, already involved in special operations. The 'guide' (**C3**) wore the basic American uniform and was

armed with a Garand rifle: he had a blue scarf, one of the agreed recognition signs, and left his chin-strap loose, ready to remove his helmet, another recognition sign. At this time the element of surprise was lost and his 'special' rôle was already meaningless.

*D: Kaiserbarracke, 18 December:*
*D1:SdKfz 250/7, SS-Panzer-Aufklärungs-Abteilung 1*
This le SPW SdKfz 250/7 was a mortar carrier sub-type which mounted an 8cm GrW34 tube; it was issued to the fourth platoon of some Panzer-Aufklärungs-Kompanie, to support the other platoons in action with fire from its mortar. This particular vehicle had the *neu* body which had entered production in 1943 after the decision to simplify the construction of the SdKfz 250: from 19 the number of main armoured plates had been reduced to nine. Waiting for the order to move, this SdKfz 250/7 of 3.Kompanie (SS-Obersturmführer Manfred Coblenz), SS-Panzer-Aufklärungs-Abtei-

**Another view of the Panther/M10 coded 'B7', knocked out by a bazooka near the Warche bridge at Malmédy, 21 December; Oberfeldwebel Bachmann and all but one of his crew from Panzer-Regiment 11, 6.Pz-Div. were killed as they tried to make their way back across the bridge on foot. (La Gleize Museum)**

lung 1 (SS-Sturmbannführer Gustav Knittel) was stopped by the side of the road at Kaiserbarracke, the mortar protected from the misty rain under a tarpaulin, as SS-Oberscharführer Persin walked past towards his own Schwimmwagen. The vehicle was in factory dark yellow finish and displayed the German cross on both sides of the hull; it was camouflaged with foliage attached all over the vehicle.

*D2: Schwimmwagen, SS-Panzer-Aufklärungs-Abteilung 1*
Another famous picture that has been wrongly captioned: in many publications, the passenger of this Schwimmwagen has been identified as Peiper himself, but this is incorrect. This man was only

an SS-Unterscharführer, whereas Peiper was an SS-Obersturmbannführer—and anyway, he never passed this spot in December 1944. This Schwimmwagen, belonging to 2.Kompanie (SS-Obersturmführer Walter Leidreiter) of SS-Panzer-Aufklärungs-Abteilung 1, stopped in front of the signpost at Kaiserbarracke. The famous photo was in fact a staged picture, as the photographer had persuaded these two NCOs to pose for a shot which would be captioned 'checking a map well inside territory formerly held by the enemy'! Immediately before taking the photo the war correspondent had proceeded to straighten the signpost, using a Mauser 98K rifle to counter-balance the half-dismantled Malmédy sign, and removing the upper American notice reading '202 ORD DEPOT FWD'. The vehicle had a Panzerfaust stored vertically behind the driver's seat in case of encounter with a heavier enemy.

All six SdKfz 138/1s from 13.(IG) Kompanie, SS-PzGren-Rgt.2 reached La Gleize, and were abandoned there after the battle. Here Capt. Benton of the US Army Air Force examines one of the 15cm sIG 33 guns near the village church: cf.Plate F.

*E: Ligneuville, 18 December:*

*E1: PzKpfw VI Ausf.B Tiger, schwere SS-Panzer-Abteilung 501*

Tiger '222' is without doubt one of the best-known, if not *the* best-known Tiger II, as the picture showing it passing at Kaiserbarracke with its load of Fallschirmjäger has been published in every book dealing with Panzers of the late Second World War! Strangely, this particular Tiger II was photographed at four different locations by the German Kriegsberichter, and at a fifth place—where it was finally abandoned—by American or local photographers. We can thus see Tiger '222' at Tondorf on the eve of the battle; then on the move on 18 December with a group of Fallschirmjäger from F.J.Rgt.9 standing on its deck, first at Deidenberg, then at Kaiserbarracke, and at the entry of Ligneuville waiting for the order to take the road towards Stavelot. On the next day it would be hit by American TD shots at the southern end of the Stavelot bridge and abandoned there, the

crew escaping unharmed through the turret rear hatch under cover of darkness. Tiger '222' belonged to the second platoon, commanded by SS-Untersturmführer Georg Hantusch, in 2.Kompanie, commanded by SS-Hauptsturmführer Rolf Möbius; it was painted in the 'ambush scheme'.

*E2: PzKpfw V Ausf.G Panther, SS-Panzer-Regiment 1*
At least 15 Panthers would be left in La Gleize and Stoumont after the withdrawal of Kampfgruppe Peiper. This Panther Ausf.G belonged to SS-Panzer-Regiment 1; it was a Panzerbefehlswagen, a command tank, equipped with an extra radio set (either the FuG7 or the FuG8) in addition to the usual FuG5. The exact meaning of the '002' marking is uncertain, but this tank was probably the second vehicle in the regimental staff group, and as such it would have been the mount of SS-

Kampfgruppe Peiper left seven Tiger II tanks in or near La Gleize. Tiger '204' was one of them, but was later driven northwards by these American engineers, who tried to reach the railway station at Spa. The tank broke down near Ruy, and would move no further; instead, Tiger '332' was salvaged at Coo, and shipped to Aberdeen Proving Grounds. See Plate H.

Hauptsturmführer Hans Gruhle. Like most of the regiment's tanks, Panther '002' was painted in the three-colour scheme, but in a somewhat rare 'striped' fashion, and displayed only a few small-size markings: a small cross and '002' painted in black on each side of the turret. In the background an SdKfz 234/2 Puma of the staff company, SS-Panzer-Aufklärungs-Abteilung 1, could be seen; it was camouflaged with red-brown 'tiger stripes' painted over the dark yellow factory colour. The recce battalion had 13 heavy recce armoured cars on 12 December, among these a few Pumas; three Pumas would be found in La Gleize after the withdrawal of Kampfgruppe Peiper.

*F: La Gleize, 19 December, morning:*
*F1: PzKpfw IV Ausf.J, SS-Panzer-Regiment 1*
1.SS-Panzer-Division had 34 Panzer IVs with the 6. and 7.Kompanie of its Panzer-Regiment 1 at the beginning of the offensive. These companies were among the vanguards of Kampfgruppe Peiper, and

some of their Panzer IVs went on westwards to fight at Stoumont and La Gleize. This Ausf.J belonged to 7.Kompanie, and displayed its number '713' in black, outlined with white. The basic dark factory yellow ochre has been overpainted with sprayed green and red-brown secondary colours. The German cross was 'empty', having only the four white outlining 'corners'. The vehicle had no Zimmerit except on the side skirts, which were all present when this picture was taken—quite a rare occurrence. The crew wore their black Panzer uniform, but this could only be seen at the collar and cap as they had donned over it the reed-green denim uniform; following the Heer, which had introduced it in May 1941, the Waffen-SS adopted this for wear by armoured vehicle crews, for protective and camouflage purposes and for wear as a summer uniform.

## F2: SdKfz 138/1, SS-Panzergrenadier-Regiment 2

Each of the two Panzergrenadier regiments of a Panzer-Division 44 (a division based on the 1944 organisation) was supposed to have a company of six self-propelled infantry guns. At the beginning of December 1944 the 13.(IG)Kompanie of SS-Panzergrenadier-Regiment 2 had its full complement of six guns, and its counterpart in SS-Panzergrenadier-Regiment 1 had five guns; the former company was engaged with Kampfgruppe Peiper and the latter with Kampfgruppe Hansen. Both these companies were equipped with the SdKfz 138/1, which mounted a 15cm s.IG 33 gun on a PzKpfw 38(t) chassis. The six guns with Kampfgruppe Peiper backed the Kampfgruppe attack by shelling Stavelot early on 18 December, and Stoumont the next morning; all six were abandoned in La Gleize when the Kampfgruppe withdrew. The basic dark yellow has been 'stamped' with splotches of dark green and red-brown, and the vehicles were heavily camouflaged with foliage. It seems that they carried no marking at all, except possibly the division's shield on the front armour.

## G: Stoumont, 19 December:

### G1: PzKpfw V Ausf.G Panther, SS-Panzer-Regiment 1

1. and 2. Kompanie of SS-Panzer-Regiment 1 were equipped with Panthers as part of Kampfgruppe Peiper: they could field 37 Panthers at the beginning of the offensive. This Panther Ausf.G of 2.Kompanie was found in La Gleize after the withdrawal of the Kampfgruppe. It had no

**This Jagdpanzer IV/70 of SS-Panzer-Jäger-Abteilung 1 was the mount of SS-Untersturmführer Otto Holst, commander of the battalion's 1st Battery. It ended up in the Amblève when SS-Standartenführer Hansen ordered the unit to attempt to cross the weak bridge at Petit-Spai: cf. Plate I.**

'For you the war is over . . .' One can imagine the comment of SS-Stubaf. Josef Diefenthal, commander of III/SS-PzGren-Rgt.2, as prisoners of the US 119th Infantry are marched away at Stoumont, 19 December: see Plate L.

Zimmerit, and displayed the standard three-colour camouflage; it had small German crosses on the front hull sides, and the number '221' was in white-outlined black figures. It carried three rows of track links as protection on each of the turret sides, and a lot of branches as additional camouflage. This is a somewhat rare vehicle, as only a handful were produced as trial production vehicles for testing the new suspension, with the steel-rimmed 'silent-block' wheels that were to be standardised on the Ausf.F in 1945. A spare road wheel could be seen on the engine deck.

*G2: Wirbelwind, schwere SS-Panzer-Abteilung 501*
The document '*Auffrischung der Panz.Div. im Westen*' indicates that 1.SS-Panzer-Division was supposed to have 16 Flakpanzers with its Panzer regiment in

late 1944: eight 37mm 'Ostwind' from 10.(Flak) Kompanie of SS-Panzer-Regiment 1, and eight quadruple 20mm 'Wirbelwind' from the attached schwere SS-Panzer-Abteilung 501. We do not know how many 'Wirbelwind' were actually fielded by schwere SS-Panzer-Abteilung 501, but 1.SS-Panzer-Division reported having their eight 'Ost-wind' at the beginning of December 1944. One thing certain is that we have identified three 'Wirbelwind' along the route followed by Kampf-gruppe Peiper, but no 'Ostwind'. This 'Wirbel-wind' was pictured in Stoumont, where its crew lent a hand to the grenadiers during the fighting on the morning of 19 December; either because they were already low on 20mm ammunition, or because the target was obviously of no importance, they fired with rifles and sub-machine guns. The vehicle had Zimmerit paste on the hull only; it had no side skirts, and was painted in the three-colour camouflage, with no markings apart from a small German cross on both sides.

*H: La Gleize, 20 December:*

*H1: PzKpfw VI Ausf.B Tiger, schwere SS-Panzer-Abteilung 501*

To replace the missing II.Abteilung in its SS-Panzer-Regiment 1, 1.SS-Panzer-Division was assigned schwere SS-Panzer-Abteilung 501, which was then quite naturally involved with Kampfgruppe Peiper. Thirty Tigers have been attributed to schwere SS-Panzer-Abteilung 501 in November, but on 10 December this unit could field only 15 Tiger IIs; a further 30 were then noted as being in the process of delivery, and it could be that half of them actually reached the front before 17 December, as the situation maps for that day show 30 Tigers with 1.SS-Panzer-Division. Tank '204' was one of the six Tigers which succeeded in reaching the La Gleize area. In position in an orchard at the edge of the village, it covered the north-east approaches. Painted in the 'ambush scheme' (as were all the 15 Tigers possessed by schwere SS-Panzer-Abteilung 501 on the eve of the offensive), it showed the Korps insignia on the left front armour.

*H2: SdKfz 251/3 Ausf.D, SS-Panzergrenadier-Regiment 2*

'It's a long way to Tipperary, boys!', Peiper called out from his SPW to some American prisoners passing by between Stoumont and La Gleize (this actually happened at Baugnez). For most of the way, Peiper was riding in an SdKfz 251 with SS-Sturmbannführer Josef Diefenthal, the commander of III.Btl., SS-Pz.Gren.Rgt.2, the infantry unit attached to his Kampfgruppe. A medium armoured personnel carrier (an SPW), this vehicle was an SdKfz 251/3 Funkpanzerwagen Ausf.D which carried two radio sets, a FuG5 and a FuG8. Painted in standard three-colour camouflage, it displayed no number, but the German cross was marked on both sides of the hull and the 1.SS-Panzer-Division insignia on the upper left corner of the front armour plate. Testimony to the poor roads in the area, a towing cable was kept attached in front of the vehicle and was stored wound around the two towing hooks. Like most of the vehicles of Kampfgruppe Peiper, this SPW has been liberally camouflaged with branches.

*I: Trois Ponts, 20–21 December:*

*I1: Hummel, SS-Panzer-Artillerie-Regiment 1*

1.SS-Panzer-Division was supposed to have a whole battalion of its SS-Panzer-Artillerie-Regiment 1 equipped with self-propelled artillery guns: two batteries each equipped with six 105mm 'Wespe' and one battery equipped with six 150mm 'Hummel'. The division was actually very poor in this respect, and on 3 December it reported having only one 'Wespe' and no 'Hummel' at all. It

**Tiger '213', the former mount of SS-Ostuf. Rudolf Dollinger, was left in a field near Wérimont Farm at La Gleize. Saved from the cutting torch in July 1945, it was beatifully restored to its original condition, and now stands in front of the La Gleize Museum—undoubtedly the most interesting relic existing today in the whole 'Battle of the Bulge' sector.**

**The museum at La Gleize opened in 1970; it contains many authentic relics of the battle—Peiper's own mapboard, this 88mm 'Puppchen', a heavy 120mm GrW 42 mortar, a fuel drum parachuted to the surrounded Kampfgruppe, and pieces from vehicles recovered near La Gleize.**

certainly received some new equipment before 16 December, as a 'Hummel' of the division was disabled near Coo by Task Force Lovelady on the afternoon of 20 December when it tried to join Kampfgruppe Peiper then gathered in La Gleize. As far as we know, it carried no markings apart from a German cross on both side armour plates. The camouflage colours are somewhat faint, giving the impression of being much weathered: this is not consistent with the idea that this 'Hummel' has just been assigned to the division, and could be explained either by the fact that it was a battle-weary 'Hummel' just back from the workshops, or by hasty painting with over-thinned paints.

*I2: Jagdpanzer IV/70, SS-Panzerjäger-Abteilung 1*
In late 1944 these Jagdpanzer IV/70s normally equipped the tank-destroyer group of each Panzer division: the normal complement for such groups

was 21 Jagdpanzer but 1.SS-Panzer-Division had only ten Jagdpanzer IV/70 with its SS-Panzerjäger-Abteilung 1 on the eve of the offensive. The group was part of Kampfgruppe Hansen and participated in the short fight for Poteau, before moving west with the Kampfgruppe in order to back Kampfgruppe Peiper. Some Jagdpanzer IV/70s managed to negotiate the very muddy tracks leading down to the southern bank of the Amblève River at Petit-Spai. When SS-Standartenführer Hansen ordered SS-Hauptsturmführer Otto Holst, the commander of the first company of Jagdpanzer IV/70s to cross the river, the latter objected to the obviously too flimsy bridge; but his objections were brushed aside, and he attempted the bridge, only to crash down with it into the river. These vehicles had no Zimmerit paste; the dark yellow base colour had been 'stamped' with splotches of red-brown. The side skirts were all torn away during the previous hours of marching and fighting. It seems that they displayed neither markings nor numbers, but they had the normal black, German cross outlined with white.

*J: Poteau, 18 December: 2 Kompanie, SS-Panzer-grenadier-Regiment 1*

These three men were pictured at Poteau on the morning of 18 December; they were members of 2.Kompanie, SS-Panzergrenadier-Regiment 1. The SS-Rottenführer (**J1**) wore a camouflaged jacket over his field grey uniform, and a Kopfschützer—the German balaclava—around his neck. Armed with a StG 44 assault rifle, he carried the canvas triple magazine pouch peculiar to this weapon, and a leather map case. The SS-Sturmann (**J2**) also wore the 1944 four-pocket camouflaged jacket over his uniform; he carried a green canvas MP 40 magazine pouch, and a fourth magazine could be seen tucked into his belt, to which was attached a folding entrenching tool. The collar patches of his field grey tunic could be seen; and he had the Waffen-SS form of the National Emblem on the left sleeve of his camouflaged jacket—not too frequent a practice on camouflage uniform. The third grenadier (**J3**) was a simple SS-Schütze who wore an older 'pullover' camouflage smock over his uniform; he had a camouflage cover on his helmet, and a balaclava under it. He was armed with an S1Kb 455(a), 'a' standing for 'amerikanisch': a captured M1 carbine. He had also 'liberated' some American Lucky Strike cigarettes.

*K: Stoumont, 19 December: 1/SS-Panzer-Regiment 1*

The commander of I.Abteilung, SS-Panzer-Regiment 1, SS-Sturmbannführer Werner Pötschke, was photographed with two of his men on the edge of Stoumont on 19 December. Pötschke (**K1**) was not wearing the black Panzer uniform but a leather outfit over his field grey uniform, a grey Army-style forage cap and mittens. His rank could be seen on the collar of his grey tunic and the shoulder straps of his leather jacket. The Ritterkreuz he won in June 1944 was dangling at his throat. Beside him (**K2**) was an SS-Untersturmführer of his battalion; a Panzer man, he wore the black Panzer jacket and the black Einheitsmütze with camouflaged trousers. The third man (**K3**) was a grenadier from the battalion of SS-Panzergrenadier-Regiment 2 attached to Kampfgruppe Peiper; he wore a smock, the trousers of the 1944 camouflage uniform, and a field grey Einheitsmütze.

*L: Stoumont, 19 December:*
*L1: SS-Stubaf. Josef Diefenthal*
*L2: Oberjäger, Fallschirm-Jäger-Regiment 9*
*L3: SS-Schütze, III/SS-Panzergrenadier-Regiment 2*

The commander of III.Btl. SS-Panzergrenadier-Regiment 2, SS-Sturmbannführer Josef Diefenthal (**L1**), was photographed in Stoumont on the morning of 19 December, urging American prisoners forward along one of the village streets. He wore a sheepskin jacket, camouflage trousers and a grey 'old style officers' field cap'. The jacket had no shoulder straps, but his rank could be seen on the tunic collar patch. The second man (**L2**) was an Oberjäger from the group of paratroopers from F.J.Rgt.9, 3.Fallschirm-Jäger-Division which had followed Kampfgruppe Peiper as far as La Gleize and Stoumont. He wore the paratrooper helmet with the Luftwaffe decal, the usual paratrooper camouflaged smock, and blue-grey trousers; he was armed with a Gew 43 automatic rifle, and a canvas double magazine pouch was strapped to his belt. The third man (**L3**) was an SS-Schütze from Diefenthal's battalion; a machine gunner, he was carrying his MG 42 and two ammunition boxes attached together over his right shoulder. He wore a balaclava round his neck, and a camouflaged 1944 jacket over his field grey uniform.

---

### Notes sur les planches en couleur

**A1** L'un des cinq StuG III Ausf.G prêtés à l'unité Skorzeny, conduite par la schwere Panzerjäger-Abteilung 655 et camouflé uniquement par un blindage latéral modifié et par une peinture gris olivâtre assortie de fausses insignes américaines blanches. **A2** Probablement, ce véhicule à chenilles accompagnait des véhicules blindés de la 2.Pz.-Div. ou de la 90.PzGren.-Div. transférés à la Panzerbrigade 150 de Skorzeny.

**B1, B2** A noter le camouflage de la plaque métallique, la fausse peinture et les fausses insignes de l'armée des Etats-Unis sur ces chars Panther Ausf.G. que Skorzeny fit passer pour des 'M10 tank destroyers' lors de la bataille de Malmédy. Le char marqué 'B4' fut endommagé par une mine tout en menant l'attaque; le 'B7', quant à lui, fut détruit par un bazooka après la traversée du pont de Warche, et tous les membres de l'équipage à l'exception d'un seul furent tués alors qu'ils se précipitaient à la recherche d'un abri.

### Farbtafeln

**A1** Einer von fünf an Skorzenys Einheit ausgeliehenen *StuG III Ausf.G*, bemannt mit der *Schweren Panzerjäger-Abt. 655* und getarnt lediglich durch eine modifizierte Seitenpanzerung und olivgrüne Farbe mit falschen amerikanischen Markierungen in weiss. **A2** Dieses alte Halbkettenfahrzeug begleitete wahrscheinlich die Fahrzeugbesatzungen der *2.Pz.-Div.* oder der auf Skorzenys *Panzerbrigade 150* übertragenen *90.PzGren.-Div.*

**B1, B2** Man beachte die Metallplatten-'Tarnung' und die falschen US Army Markierungen und Farben auf diesen Panzern der Marke *Panther Ausf.G*, in der Verkleidung von '*M10 Panzerzerstörern*' von Skorzeny bei der Schlacht von Malmédy eingesetzt. Der mit 'B4' bezeichnete Panzer (oben) stiess bei der Anführung des Angriffs auf eine Mine; 'B7' wurde nach der Überquerung der Warche-Brücke von einer Panzerbüchse getroffen, wobei alle bis auf ein Besatzungsmitglied bei der Flucht getötet wurden.

**C1** Le SS-Hstuf. von Foelkersoam portait l'uniforme SS à double face hiver/camouflage lorsqu'il dirigea la Kampfgruppe X de Skorzeny le 21 décembre. Son Ritterkreuz datait de l'époque où il figurait dans l'unité 'Brandenburg' en 1942. **C2** L'Oblt. Deier dirigeait la troupe Panther/'M10' de Skorzeny; avant le combat, il avait coutume de porter des vêtements américains par-dessus son uniforme Panzer habituel. **C3** L'un des 'guides spéciaux', entièrement habillé d'un ensemble américain; l'écharpe bleue était l'un des signes de reconnaissance.

**D1** L'un des porte-mortiers de la 3. Kompanie, SS-Pz.-Aufkl.-Abt.1 'LAH', qui s'apprête à avancer avec la colonne de Peiper. **D2** Cette photo célèbre indique à tort qu'il s'agit de Peiper lui-même, mais en réalité, les témoignages visuels de cette scène montrent le véhicule de deux gradés faisant partie de la 2. Kompanie de l'unité de reconnaissance blindée 'LAH'.

**E1** De nombreuses photos du texte montrent ce char en différents endroits alors qu'il transporte, le plus souvent, des parachutistes; le '222', assorti du type de peinture dit 'embuscade', fut abandonné au pont de Stavelot après avoir été touché par des tirs de chars destroyers américains le 19 décembre. **E2** Il s'agit peut-être du char du SS-Hstuf. Gruh... aux rayures inhabituelles est l'un de... après le retrait de la Kampfgruppe...

**F1** Ce char de la 7. Kompanie... couleurs; il y a lieu de remarquer que... côtés du blindage. Les membres de l'... en denim par-dessus leur uniforme... du régiment restèrent avec Peiper ju... La Gleize. Remarquer les taches de...

**G1** Le '221', autre Panther aband... éléments d'une petite série de véhicu... adopté de manière générale en 1945... où son équipage combattit au mo... véhicule est l'un des trois—au moi... certitude à la Kampfgruppe Peiper.

**H1** L'un des chars Tiger—probabl... avec la Kampfgruppe, ce '204' fut l'... à noter le camouflage 'embuscade'... Peiper lui-même parvint presque jus... était accompagné du SS-Stubaf. Di...

**I1** Endommagé près de Coo le 20 déc... à La Gleize, ce véhicule était couver... peut s'agir d'un véhicule ancien e... véhicules, qui possèdent, en guise de... contours, ne semblent avoir possédé... L'un d'eux, commandé par le SS-Ha... trop léger qui enjambait l'Amblève...

**J1** Jeune gradé SS portant la ves... uniforme feldgrau; toque de laine... cartouchières caractéristiques pour le... avec un MP.40, porte le même unifor... la manche n'était pas très courante à... blouse de camouflage plutôt ancien... carabine M1 dérobée à l'armée amé...

**K1** Le SS-Stubaf. Pötschke est ici ph... cuir—la couleur grise est incertaine... **K2** Uniforme SS-Panzer noir habi... camouflage. **K3** Cet homme por... Panzerfaust. Les trois hommes furen...

**L1** Le SS-Stubaf. Diefenthal, photog... faisait conduire verse l'arrière des p... peau de mouton et un 'bonnet de ca... se trouvait **L2**, un parachutiste du... raison uniquement du fusil autom... bataillon de Diefenthal, portant la v... MG.42 ainsi que ses coffres.

**C1** SS-Hstuf. von Foelkersoam trug die umkehrbare SS-Winteruniform, als er am 21. Dezember Skorzenys *Kampfgruppe X* anführte; sein *Ritterkreuz* erhielt er 1942 für seinen Dienst bei einer *'Brandenburg'*-Einheit. **C2** Oblt. Deier befehligte Skorzenys *Panther/'M10'*-Einheit; vor der Schlacht zog er US-Kleidung über seine normale Panzeruniform. **C3** Einer der 'Spezialführer', ganz in amerikanische Ausrüstung gekleidet; das blaue Halstuch war ein Erkennungszeichen.

**D1** Ein Granatträger der *3.Kompanie, SS-Pz.-Aufkl.-Abt.1 'LAH'* wartet auf den Vorstoss mit Peipers Kolonne. **D2** Eine berühmte falsche Zuweisung gibt dies als Peiper selbst aus, aber die Bilder zeigen das Fahrzeug zweier Unteroffiziere der *2.Kompanie* der bewaffneten *'LAH'*-Aufklärungseinheit.

**E1** Viele Fotos im Text zeigen diesen Panzer an verschiedenen Punkten, gewöhnlich mit Fallschirmspringern an Bord; Nr. 222, bemalt mit dem sogenannten 'Hinterhalt'-Farbenschema, wurde bei der Stavelot-Brücke zurückgelassen, nachdem das Fahrzeug am 19. Dezember von US Panzerzerstörern angeschossen worden war. **E2** Möglicherweise der Panzer des SS-Hstuf. Gruhle des Regimentsstabs; dieser Panther mit seinen ungewöhnlichen S... zurückgelassenen Fahrzeugen, nachdem ...ückgezogen hatte.

...nie trägt das übliche Dreifarbenschema; man ...npanzerung befindliche *Zimmerit*-Tünche. Die ...eitsanzüge über den schwarzen Uniformen. **F2** ...IG)Kompanie blieben bis zum Ende an Peipers ...en bis La Gleize Feuerschutz. Man beachte die

...eize zurückgelassener Panther, ist ein Exemplar ...smodellen mit diesen Rädern, die 1945 bei der ...wurden. **G2** Dieses in Stoumont fotografierte ...n 19. Dezember mit kleinen Waffen kämpfte, ...mplaren dieses Typs, die mit Bestimmtheit der ...erden können.

...ch 30 *Tiger*-Panzern der *Kampfgruppe*, erreichte ...La Gleize; man beachte das 'Hinterhalt'- ...n des *1.SS-Pz.-Korps 'LAH'*. **H2** Peiper fuhr ...n diesem Halbkettenfahrzeug mit SS-Stubaf.

...zu Peiper in La Gleize zu stossen, am 20. ...ine auffällig schwache Tarnung und war ...plar. **I2** Diese zehn Farhzeuge mit klar ...ausser des Hakenkreuzekeine anderen ...Holz kommandierte Exemplar brach durch ...Amblève.

...acke von 1944 über seiner feldgrauen Uniform; ...üstung die auffälligen Magazinbeutel für das ...mit einer *MP.40* trägt eine ähnliche Uniform; ...el war zu diesem Zeitpunkt nicht mehr typisch. ...Tarnkittel anstelle der Jacke von 1944 ist mit ...der US Army bewaffnet.

...beim Einsatz mit einem (vermuthlich grauen) ...e im Armeestil. **K2** Die übliche schwarze SS- ...hosen in Tarnmuster getragen. **K3** Älterer ...le drei Männer wurden am 19. Dezember in

...Dezember in Stoumont fotografiert, drängt ...ück. Diefenthal trug diese Schaffelljacke und ...lmütze. In der Nähe stand **L2**, ein Fall- ...öhnlich an seiner Ausrüstung war lediglich der ...IG-Schütze aus Diefenthals Bataillon, hier mit ...und einem *MG.42* mit Munitionskästen.